Linen Crafts

40 Projects for Home & Body

I dedicate this book to my mother.

Editor: Jennifer Eiss
Interior designer: Anne Schlaffmann
Cover designer: Nancy Leonard

Library of Congress Cataloging-in-Publication Data: Le Maux, Florence.
Linen crafts : 40 projects for home & body / by Florence Le Maux   ;
photographs by Claire Curt.
p. cm.
ISBN 1-58479-496-8
1. Textile crafts. 2. Linen. I. Title.

TT699.L46 2006
746'.0411--dc22

2005031331

Copyright © 2004 Editions Minerva, Geneve (Suisse)

Published in 2006 by Stewart, Tabori & Chang
An imprint of Harry N. Abrams, Inc.

The text of this book was composed in Bliss and Helvetica Neue

Printed and bound in China

10 9 8 7 6 5 4 3 2 1

HNA
harry n. abrams, inc.
a subsidiary of La Martinière Groupe

115 West 18th Street
New York, NY 10011
www.stcbooks.com

Florence Le Maux

Linen Crafts

40 Projects for Home & Body

Photographs by Claire Curt

STC Craft | A Melanie Falick Book

Stewart, Tabori & Chang
NEW YORK

Preface

Of all textiles, linen is the most ancient, and the noblest.

The product of a thousand-year-old agricultural tradition, this natural fiber is a study in contrasts; linen's fibers wick moisture away, making it dry, airy, and cool in the summer, and in the winter it insulates efficiently for cozy comfort. Its hypoallergenic and thermal qualities make linen an ideal material for clothing and household items. Many have claimed to sleep more deeply and serenely in linen sheets.

The fashion world and its designers have embraced linen for clothing because of its natural adaptability, which assures elegance without affectation; even wrinkled, it possesses an insouciant style. In this volume you will find a few basic articles of summer clothing that you can personalize or modify as you please to coordinate with your wardrobe, or adapt to suit a particular occasion.

Natural linen has been all but forgotten in the wardrobes of little ones. This is a pity, as some weaves can be extremely soft, and its durability, its natural moisture absorption, and its hypoallergenic qualities make it a natural in projects for babies.

In the area of home decor, linen currently reigns supreme. In its various manifestations, from raw linen to more refined fabrics, it is equally at home in traditional or contemporary interiors, in the country or in the city, integrating itself as well into a sophisticated city apartment as into a rustic country house.

Linen's neutral yet naturally warm coloring complements a diverse number of luxurious materials—velvet, leather, lace, and so on—to superb effect. It easily lends itself to creative modification, from dyeing to collage, painting, or embroidery.

This book gives me the opportunity to explore and appreciate all the virtues of this extraordinary material. Linen has long intrigued me and spurred a desire to create—and the result is a series of projects that are very easy to make at home, since none require specialized knowledge of sewing or craft techniques.

My enthusiasm for linen has always been unbounded, and I am delighted to share it here with readers, who now can give their own creativity free rein in these projects.

Florence Le Maux

The Different Kinds of Linen

Natural linen

Since it is not dyed, it is not uniform in color, but ranges through various shades of beige. There are numerous types of linen fabric: it may be fine or heavy, quite crisp or more flowing, very soft (more often used for clothing) or more rugged in texture (as with many textured linens popular for upholstery or interior decoration). The price can double for linen of especially fine quality. But from a purely aesthetic point of view the price is of no importance; the coarser fabrics can have a lovely effect. Most kinds of linen are easily found in all the fabric stores.

Linen used for embroidery or hemstitching effects should be very regular in its weave. Often such fabrics will be identified by the spacing of its thread; 28-thread linen, for example, has 28 threads per inch.

The most important characteristic when choosing natural linen is that it be suitable for the specific intended use, in interior decoration just as in clothing.

It is best to wash linen before working with it, as it shrinks. Laundering will also soften the fabric, and cause it to fade somewhat. However, when it is used for things that will not be washed afterward (like the menu frame on page 61, the Moroccan pouffe on page 86, and the antiqued flower painting on page 109), you can skip the washing stage so you do not alter its look or texture.

Linen for clothing

These fabrics are fine and soft. Linen is most often used in summer clothing, so it is most easily available at the beginning of spring. Linen for clothing can be found in a large variety of colors, varying in different shops and with seasonal fashion.

Clothing-quality linen can also be used for interior decoration (as in the gilded centerpiece cloth on page 54).

Certain linens used have an irregular, slubbed weave, similar to that of raw silk (see the reversible skirt on page 15, for example).

Linen for interior design

Linen used for upholstery, drapes, and so on is often heavier, more rugged, and more textural than that used in apparel. It can be found in many variations, natural, dyed, or printed, on the shelves of furniture stores. For most of the projects here, I have preferred to use white or ecru linen and dye it when needed.

Special embroidery linen, most commonly with 28 threads per inch, can be found in white, ecru, and several neutral colors; of the highest quality, this cloth's regularity makes it perfect for embroidery or hemstitching.

Specialty linens

—*Raw linen* is very similar to jute in appearance. The natural fibers of the flax plant can be seen in its weave. Its rustic appearance gives it great charm and intrigue (see the log carrier on page 107, and the weekend throw on page 110). Raw linen should not be machine-washed, because it will shed, fray, and clog the washing machine's filter.

—*Polished linen*, fine in texture, is usually colored, and treated to give it a somewhat glossy finish.

—*Coated linen*, also sometimes referred to as waxed or oilskin linen, is naturally resistant to moisture and dirt. It is useful for such things as the place mats on page 53, as it is easily wiped clean.

Linen thread, string, and cord

Notions stores offer a variety of linen threads: for sewing, in many colors, thinner or thicker depending on its use (fine for sewing, thicker for attaching beads, about .5 to 1 mm in diameter).

Linen string about 1.5 or 2 mm in diameter can be found in department stores, in the kitchen section, as well as in craft shops.

Craft stores stock linen cord in various thicknesses, as well as different textures, for a range of looks, from smooth to rough.

Contents

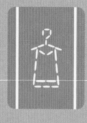

Fashion

?

Easy

Time: 3 hours

Size: 8/10 (see patterns for 6/8 and 10/12)

Materials

- **20-in. x 60-in. piece of fine, light rose linen**
- **60 in. of rose-colored bias tape**
- **assorted linen thread**
- **needles**
- **pins**
- **scissors**
- **sewing machine**

See pattern, page 122

A Dancer's Wrap Top

Instructions

- Transfer the pattern to actual size (see General Techniques, page 156) and cut out. Fold the linen rectangle in two along the long side and match the fabric fold to the area indicated on the pattern. Pin the pattern to the cloth and cut both pieces of material along the pattern lines without cutting the fold. Unfold the material to show the entire wrap. Sew the front and back part of each shoulder together along the back side.

- Hem the bottom of the wrap.

- Hem the rest of the wrap—that is, from the neckline to the points—by hand.

- Hem the armholes and notch them ⅜ in., as indicated on the pattern; fold the "tabs" under and stitch the hem.

- Sew the bias tape on along the inside of each armhole to conceal the hem. Stitch the seam only along one side of the bias (the side toward the exterior edge of the armhole).

A delightful wrap, this is very easy to make. For an even more elegant look, use black linen with a border of lace or sequins.

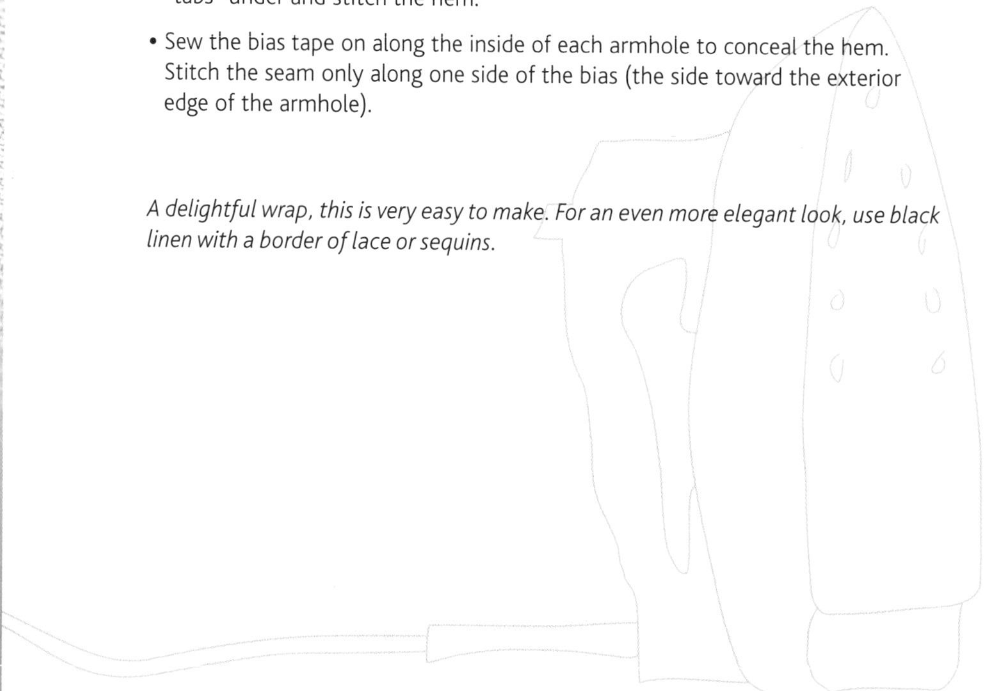

Your Professional Cleaner

A Reversible Skirt

Very easy
Time: 2 hours
One size

Instructions

- Transfer the pattern to actual size (see General Techniques, page 156) and cut out.

- Place the pattern on the linen, pin, and cut. Repeat the operation with the Liberty fabric.

- Hem the linen and the Liberty fabric along one of the long sides, and between A and B on the opposite side.

- Mark the pleats as indicated on the pattern and the diagrams. Pin in place, then stitch the pleats. Iron flat.

- Attach one of the two parts of each snap beside each pleat of the Liberty fabric, as marked, and attach the other parts by the pleats of the linen.

- Place the linen and Liberty fabric on top of each other, right side to right side.

- Sew together the sides of the skirt, and the top up to A and B. Turn inside out.

- Cut the ribbon into two pieces and attach a piece to each upper corner of the skirt.

You can make this skirt as short or as long as you like; simply adjust the dimensions of the linen and Liberty fabric.

Material

- 34 3/8-in. x 38 3/8-in. piece of natural linen (see page 7)
- 34 3/8-in. x 39 1/4-in. piece of Liberty print fabric
- 40 in. of grosgrain ribbon to match the Liberty fabric
- 2 large snaps
- thread
- needles
- pins
- scissors
- sewing machine
- iron

See pattern and diagrams, pages 122–23

Somewhat difficult

Time: 5 hours for the tunic and
5 hours for the embroidery

Size: 6/8 (see patterns for
8/10 and 10/12)

Materials

- 48-in. x 56-in. piece of fine
  lavender linen
- 3 skeins of DMC six-strand
  embroidery floss: dark gray
  (article 844), light buff (article
  3866), lavender (article 161)
- 1 lavender zipper, about 10 in.
  long
- erasable textile pen
- thread to match the linen
- needles
- pins
- sewing machine
- iron

See patterns, page 124

Embroidery stitch to use:
Maltese tassel (see page 158)

A Fringed Tunic

Instructions

The Tunic

- Transfer the pattern to actual size (see General Techniques, page 156) and cut out.

- For the front of the tunic: Fold the linen rectangle in half along the long side and match the linen fold to the dotted line indicated on the pattern. Warning: Be sure to position the material on the pattern so there is still room for the other parts of the tunic. Pin the pattern to the linen and cut out, following the pattern, through both layers of fabric, leaving the fold uncut. Unfold the linen to reveal the entire front of the tunic.

- For the back of the tunic: With the rest of the linen, repeat the directions above, using the pattern for the back part of the tunic.

- For the sleeves: Place the pattern for the arms on a piece of the linen, pin, and cut. Repeat the operation to make two sleeves.

- Place the collar patterns for the front and back of the tunic on the linen, pin, and cut out.

- On the front of the tunic, mark the darts for the chest and sew them on the back side. Hem the edges of the sleeves.

- Assemble the front collar and the front of the tunic, right side to right side (see pattern for placement), and sew together 2 in. from the edge. Turn over. Assemble and sew together the back collar and the back of the tunic in the same manner.

- Assemble the front and back parts of the tunic together, right side to right side; baste, and then stitch along the shoulders.

- Baste the sleeves to the armholes, without pleating. Sew on the back side.

- Fold the tunic at the shoulders, right side to right side. Sew the right side from under the arm, down to A. Sew the sleeves. On the left side, baste, then sew on, the zipper. Finish the seam down to A. Hem each side of the vents, from A to B, and hem along the bottom of the tunic.

- On the back side, mark the darts on the back and front. Baste, try on for fit, and adjust the darts, then sew.

- Turn the tunic right side out and iron.

The Maltese Tassels for the Sleeves and the Neckline

- With a textile pen, draw a 2⅜-in. line for each tassel along the neckline and around the sleeve cuffs.

- Thread a needle with the light brown embroidery floss, using six strands, and bring the needle through the middle of the marked line; pull the floss through, leaving a ¾-in. strand of thread. Bring the needle out again on the left side of the line, and enter again on the far right side underneath the strand. Bring it out again at the center. Cut this second strand to the same length as the first. The ¾ in. of floss left will make a little tassel.

- Continue in the same manner, alternating thread color.

You can accentuate the oriental quality of this tunic by embroidering with metallic thread.

An Umbel-Motif Stole

Very easy
Time: 3 hours

Instructions

• Hem the four sides of the linen rectangle.

• Place the linen over the umbel motifs and copy them onto the material with the textile pencil.

• Cut the linen thread into pieces, in lengths to match the stems and large blades of the umbels.

• Attach the linen-string stems, as well as three or four blades for each umbel, to the fabric with the lamé thread, using the Boulogne stitch (see legend, "Linen string," for placement on motif).

• Fasten a sequin to the end of each blade (see legend, "Sequins").

• Embroider the small blades where indicated (see legend, "Glass seed beads") with the seed beads on the polyester thread.

By using linen of a darker color (burgundy, black, taupe . . .) and spangles instead of sequins, you can also make an evening stole with dramatic flair.

Materials

• 14-in. x 68-in. piece of fine white linen

• 40 in. of linen string

• 30 sequins, more or less

• erasable textile pencil

• tube of iridescent seed beads

• thread to match the linen

• silver lamé thread

• white polyester sewing thread

• needles

• scissors

See motifs, page 125

Embroidery stitch to use: Boulogne stitch (see page 158)

Materials

- 8-in. x 40-in. piece of brown polished linen (see page 7)
- 80 in. of pink grosgrain ribbon, 1⅝ in. wide
- 12 in. hot pink nylon cord
- 2 mother-of-pearl buttons
- thread to match the linen
- needles
- pins
- scissors
- sewing machine
- iron

See patterns and diagrams, page 126

A Bohemian Pouch

Instructions

- Transfer the pattern to actual size (see General Techniques, page 156) and cut out. Place the pattern on the linen, pin, and cut (this will give you a 13¼-in. x 36-in. rectangle). Cut out and iron the darts as indicated on the pattern.

- Hem the flap of the handbag with a double fold as indicated on the pattern (hems 1, 2, 3). Hem the side opposite to the flap (hem 4), also using a double fold.

- Form a pouch by folding the rectangle in half along the line indicated on the pattern. Sew the sides ⅜ in. from the edge. Turn inside out.

- Fold the edges toward the inside, about ¾ in. on each side of the seam. Tack down the corner with a few stitches. With an iron, make creases at the bottom of the handbag, ¾ in. from each side of the seams.

- Pin the grosgrain along the entire side of the pouch, beginning and then finishing at the middle of the bottom. Petit-point the grosgrain to the pouch on each side.

- Sew the buttons onto the pouch where indicated on the pattern.

- Sew the hot pink cord to the back of the flap under the button.

- To close the pouch, wind the fluorescent thread around the buttons in a figure eight.

You can replace the grosgrain with a wide band of spangles (available from large craft shops).

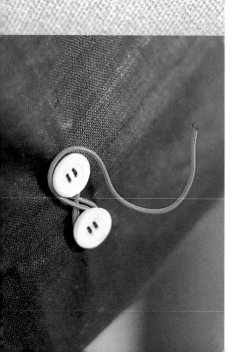

A Flower Brooch

Easy

**Time: 30 minutes,
plus one hour to dry**

Instructions

- Photocopy the two circles from the pattern and cut them out. Pin them to the linen and cut. Repeat this step three times for the large (2⅜-in.) circle and two times for the small (1⅝-in.) circle, to end with four large and three small circles.

- Cover the large ball with the plastic wrap. Paint one 2⅜-in. circle with the acrylic medium and press the circle firmly around the ball to shape it. Then paint the outside of the circle with acrylic (the circle will be coated on both sides). Allow to dry. When the acrylic is dry, carefully detach the circle from the ball. Push the middle of the circle in somewhat to give the petal shape.

- Repeat the operation with the other three 2⅜-in. circles.

- Cover the small ball with plastic wrap. Follow the instructions above for the 1⅝-in. circles.

- Sew the three small petals together to form the center of the flower (see figure 1). Sew the four large petals together to form the outer part of the flower (see figure 2).

- Thread the beads on the beige thread to form a line of beads about 4⅜ in. long. Thread three other lines of the same length. Place the line of beads along the outer edge of one of the large petals and fasten it with a straight stitch. Repeat this with the other three large petals.

- Sew the small flower center to the center of the large petal group (see figure 3). Thread 100 beads and attach this line in a spiral to the center of the small group of petals, using a straight stitch.

- Thread five lines of beads about 3¼ or 3⅝ in. long onto longer threads (about 10 in. long). Thread these five threads through the same needle, and sew them to the center of the spiral.

- Sew the brooch pin onto the back of the flower.

You can also make these flowers using dyed linen, edged with sequins instead of beads.

Materials

- 12-in. x 12-in. piece of natural linen (see page 7)

- 1 jar of acrylic binding medium, such as Liquitex Gloss Heavy Gel

- 3 tubes of pearl beige seed beads (about 400)

- 1 pin for the brooch

- plastic wrap

- 2 Styrofoam balls, 2⅜ in. and 1⅝ in. in diameter (or use a Ping-Pong ball for the small one)

- beige thread

- needles

See patterns and diagrams, page 127

Embroidery stitch to use: straight stitch (see page 158)

Very easy

Time: 2 hours

Materials

- 28-in. natural linen dishcloth, checkered in white (sold by the length)
- 52-in. waxed cord, about ¼ in. in diameter
- 2 set-it-yourself grommets (or ask a shoe-repair store to set them)
- old rubber stamps of animals (found at flea markets)
- fabric ink for stamping
- white embossing powder
- thread to match the linen
- needles
- safety pin
- pins
- scissors
- sewing machine
- source of intense heat (an iron or heat plate)

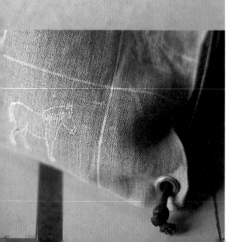

A Little Boy's Backpack

Instructions

- Make a ¾-in. hem along one of the long sides of the linen rectangle, to create a cord channel.

- Fold the rectangle in half, right side to right side. Stitch ⅜ in. from the edge. Unfold the cylinder you have just made. Flatten this cylinder again so that the seam that you have just made is in the center and no longer on the side. This will be the back of the backpack.

- On the back of the backpack, make a small opening of about ⅜ in. in the middle of the cord channel, on the outside. Oversew the opening to keep it from fraying.

- On the front of the backpack, stamp a pattern in the center of one of the squares. Immediately sprinkle with the embossing powder. Shake off the excess powder from the cloth. Heat the remaining powder by placing under a source of heat, like a hot plate or iron, for a few seconds (do not allow the heat source to touch the cloth, or it will burn). Repeat this operation for each stamp.

- At each bottom corner of the backpack, set (or have a shoe repair store set for you) a grommet through both thicknesses of cloth.

- With the safety pin, thread the cord through the channel, beginning and ending at the little opening in the back.

- Lace each end of the cord through one of the grommets and tie it in a knot on the other side so that the cord cannot slip back through the grommets. Pull the cord to close the backpack.

Try using different colors of stamp ink and embossing powder; you can also make this backpack with "alphabet" stamps.

Macramé Bracelets

Easy
Time: **30 minutes for each bracelet**

Instructions

- Hammer the nail into the middle of the board; this will act as an anchor when making the bracelets.

- Use one piece each of the linen string and the nylon string for each bracelet, swapping them each time to create different effects.

- Always begin by folding one of the pieces in two around the nail and knotting the second piece around the first to form a loop (see figure 1).

- Make the bracelets using the diagrams for macramé. Choose flat knots or square knots (see figures 2 and 3). You can also use both types of knots in one bracelet.

- While weaving, slide the beads onto the string between two knots at various intervals—every two knots, for example. You can also string together three or four beads at one time before making another knot.

- To complete the bracelets, make several knots one on top of the other to form a sort of ball; push this ball through the loop at the other end to close the bracelet. To make sure that the knot holds, place a drop of glue on it.

You can also use this technique to make a belt, though you may need to use a thicker linen cord, and brightly colored nylon climbing rope.

Materials

For each bracelet:

- 60 in. of linen string, about 1mm thick

- 60 in. of colored nylon string, about 1mm thick

- several large glass seed beads, the same color as the string (the holes must be large enough for the thread and string to pass through)

- 1 wood plank, about 6 in. x 6 in.

- 1 nail

- 1 hammer

- strong glue

See diagrams, page 127

Somewhat technical

Time: 3 hours

Materials

- 14⅜ in. x 22 in. of natural linen (see page 7)
- 14⅜ in. x 22 in. of white linen
- 4 in. of double-sided iron-on fusible webbing, such as Steam-a-Seam
- several pretty pieces of lace
- Swarovski iron-on crystals
- 2 resin handles
- thread to match the linen
- needles
- pins
- sewing machine
- scissors
- iron

See patterns, page 128

A Romantic Handbag

Instructions

- Transfer the pattern to actual size (see General Techniques, page 156) or photocopy it at 140 percent and cut it out. Fold the natural linen in two along the long side and match the fold to the line marked on the pattern. Warning: Fold the linen and position it on the pattern in such a way as to leave room for the rest of the pattern pieces. Pin the linen to the pattern and cut out both layers of material, leaving the fold uncut. Unfold the linen to show the bag in its entirety.

- Repeat the process with the white linen.

- Pin the pattern for the strap onto the natural linen and cut out. Fold the linen in a double fold as indicated on the pattern, then fold in half and sew the long side. Cut the strap into four equal pieces; fold each piece in half, and pin them to the natural linen at A, indicated on the pattern.

- Lay the two pieces of linen on top of each other, pin together, and stitch 8mm from the edge around the entire bag, leaving an opening between the two points marked A on the pattern. Turn inside out, then iron.

- Fold the bag in two, right side to right side (the white linen on the outside). Pin and sew each side of the top of the bag, along the fold line, to the base. Before the last stitch, pull slightly on the thread to bunch up the corners slightly. Finish the stitching. Turn right side out.

- Arrange the lace on the stickier side of the iron-on fusible webbing, leaving the paper backing on the other side. Seal with the iron, making sure to place a piece of parchment paper between the lace and the iron, so you can remove the surplus fusible webbing. Allow to cool and remove the paper backing from the fusible webbing. Arrange the lace motifs on the bag, with the newly exposed fusible webbing against the bag. Place a sheet of parchment paper between the iron and the material, and iron the lace to attach it to the bag.

- Arrange the Swarovski crystals on the bag, place a sheet of parchment paper over them, and iron them onto the bag. Press a few moments. Turn the bag over and heat it a little with the iron. Slide the handles into the straps.

You can also replace the resin handles with knotted muslin scarves.

A Chicken Tote

Easy

Time: 3 hours

Instructions

• Photocopy the hen and chick motifs, and cut out.

• Divide the cotton wool to make two rectangles of equal size.

• Place one linen rectangle on top of one of the large rectangles of voile. Stitch three sides: the two long sides, one short side, and part of the second short side. Turn inside out. Slide one of the cotton wool rectangles between the two pieces and finish sewing the final short side.

• Follow the above directions for the remaining two pieces of linen and voile to make the other side of the bag.

• Pin the hen and chick motifs onto the raspberry- and burgundy-colored voile and onto the double-sided iron-on fusible webbing and cut out (see diagram for the placement of the motifs).

• Place the cut-out pieces of voile on the fusible webbing, with the stickier side facing the voile, and heat-seal them with an iron. Peel away the paper backing.

• Arrange the pieces on one side of the bag, with the fusible webbing against the linen. Iron to seal them onto the bag.

• With the colored thread, stitch lines parallel to the long side of the bag, about 15mm apart, on both sides of the bag, alternating the colors and stitching through all three layers of cloth as well as the motifs themselves to quilt the bag.

• Place the two sides of the bag on top of each other, right side to ride side. Stitch along three sides (two long and one short). Turn inside out. Tuck the corners inside the bag to form the bottom of the bag and tack it with a few stitches to hold the shape (see diagram for making the bottom of the bag).

• To make the handles of the bag, cut the string into twelve pieces (six per handle).

• For each handle, braid six pieces together: begin and end each braid with a knot and leave 2 in. of string unbraided. Stitch the knots of the handles onto the exterior of the bag.

You can also make this shopping tote without the hen motif, instead crossing the lines of quilting.

Materials

• 2 rectangles, 12¾ in. x 16 in., of thick natural linen (see p.7)

• 2 rectangles, 12¾ in. x 16 in., and one rectangle, 6 in. x 12 in., of raspberry-colored voile

• 1 rectangle, 12 in. x 15¼ in., of cotton wool

• 8 in. x 20 in. of Steam-a-Seam double-sided iron-on fusible webbing

• 48 in. of heavy linen string, about 3 or 4 mm in diameter

• 4 spools of linen thread: red, anise green, green, and beige

• thread to match the linen

• needles

• pins

• scissors

• sewing machine

• iron

See diagrams and motifs, page 129

Somewhat technical

Time: 1 hour, 30 minutes for each piece

Size: 3 months (see patterns for newborn, 1 month, and 6 months)

Materials

- 32-in. x 32-in. piece of soft natural linen (see page 7)
- 32 in. x 32 in. pink poplin (or the color of your choice)
- 2 squares, 2⅜ in. x 2⅜ in., of Liberty print fabric (or a print of your choice)
- 2 pretty buttons
- 2 snaps
- 1 erasable textile pencil
- thread to match the linen
- needles
- pins
- scissors
- sewing machine
- iron

See patterns and diagrams, pages 130–131

An Elegant Ensemble

Instructions

- Transfer the patterns to actual size (see General Techniques, page 156) and cut out.

The Body

- Fold the square of linen and match the fold to the line marked on the pattern for the body. Note: Be sure to fold the linen and position the pattern in such a way as to save room for the other pieces of the ensemble. Pin the pattern onto the linen and cut, cutting through both layers of material and leaving the fold uncut.
- Repeat, using the poplin square.
- Unfold the two pieces to reveal the body in its entirety. Save the remaining material.
- Place the poplin and linen squares on top of each other, right side to right side. Sew them together about 8mm from the edge, leaving 4 in. between A and B open (see pattern; B is the symmetrical point to A).
- Turn inside out and stitch the remaining 4 in.
- Fasten a snap onto the flaps as indicated on the pattern, then a small button on top as a decoration. Tie the bottom together like a diaper.

The Flower

- On the remaining piece of poplin, cut out a 2⅜-in. x 2⅜-in. square. Fold the poplin square into four and iron. Arrange the square as shown in the diagram (that is, like a diamond) with all the loose ends together at the top. Trace a heart with the textile pencil onto the material and cut from A to B (see diagram). Unfold to reveal a flower.
- Repeat these steps with two squares of Liberty print fabric and cut a smaller heart with one and a larger heart with the other. Unfold these flowers.
- Place the three flowers on top of each other, the largest at the bottom and the smallest at the top, and petit-point them together at their center using a small button to hide the stitching. Sew one of the snap pieces to the flower and the other to the body. This flower can then be removed before washing the body.

The Slippers

• Place the pattern for the sole of the slippers onto the remaining linen piece, pin, and cut. Repeat this operation three times to end with four soles. Stack them two and two and sew a zigzag (or a straight stitch ¼ in. from the edge if your machine does not have a zigzag) around the circumference of the soles.

• Place the pattern for the upper part of the slippers onto the remaining linen, pin, and cut. Repeat the operation again to end with two upper parts.

• Follow the above directions to cut two upper slipper parts from the remaining poplin.

• Stack one poplin and one linen upper on top of each other right side to right side. Sew them together, saving the area between A and B (see pattern), then turn inside out, and sew the remaining bit between A and B.

• Position each upper part onto a sole, and sew them together using the zigzag between C and D.

• Tie the back parts together.

The Sailor's Hat

• Place the pattern for the top part of the hat onto the remaining piece of linen, pin, and cut out. Repeat five times to end with six triangles of linen. Assemble the triangles in a circle with the points at the center and sew together. Turn over to make the crown of the hat.

• Place the patterns for the sides of the hat (exterior and interior), one on the remaining linen and the other on the remaining poplin; pin, then cut. Place the linen and poplin sides on top of each other, right side to right side. Sew together from A to B (see pattern). Turn inside out.

• Pin and then sew the band to the hat, the border of the linen band against the border of the hat, then petit point (see Figure 1). Fold the band of poplin over the linen band and sew (see Figure 2). Tie the ends together.

Linen is a hypoallergenic material, but take care to choose a soft and fine (and thus somewhat more expensive) weave, since a baby's skin is very delicate and sensitive.

Easy
Time: 1 hour per animal

Materials

- 3 squares, each 12 in. x 12 in., of natural linen (see page 7)
- 12-in. x 12-in. square of fine sky blue felt
- 12-in. x 12-in. square of fine green felt
- 12-in. x 12-in. square of fine orange felt
- synthetic cotton wool (to fill the animals)
- 3 spools of thread to match the felt (sky blue, green, orange)
- Chinese black linen thread
- large sharp needle
- needles
- pins
- scissors
- sewing machine

See patterns, page 131

Little Stuffed Animals

Instructions

- Photocopy the bear, cow, and chick patterns at 200 percent, and cut out.

The Bear

- Place the body and head patterns on a square of linen, pin, and cut out.

- Repeat with the felt, then place the patterns for the ears, paws, and snout on the felt, and cut out.

- Place the large circle of linen and the large circle of felt on top of each other (to make the body) and pin them together. Stitch them together ¼ in. from the edge, leaving an open gap of about 1⅝ in. Turn inside out. Fill with cotton wool, then sew the opening closed.

- Repeat the process using the two small circles.

- With thread matching the felt, stitch the paws, snout, and ears onto the small circle.

- With the Chinese black thread, make the eyes: Thread a length of thread onto a large, sharp needle and make a large knot ¼ in. from the tip of the thread. Push the needle into the small circle in the position of one of the eyes and bring it back out at the other eye, about ¾ in. away. Make a large knot on the other end near the material and cut the remaining thread.

- Sew three claws with the black thread, hiding the knots.

- Attach the head to the body with several strong stitches.

- In the same way, make the cow, using the green felt, and the chick, using the orange felt.

A Quilted Baby Blanket

Easy
Time: 3 hours

Instructions

- Stack the linen on top of the poplin, right side to right side. Sew three and a half sides on the back, ⅜ in. from the edge. Turn inside out. Place the cotton batten inside and finish sewing the remaining side by hand.

- Trace the heart motif, cut it out, and transfer it to the linen nine times, as indicated on the diagram. Draw the straight lines from the points of the hearts.

- Matching the colors on the diagram, embroider along the straight lines and hearts, using a running stitch and passing through all layers of material to quilt the throw. Make the stitches about ⅜ in. long, spaced ¼ in. apart.

For a warmer throw, you can replace the poplin with velvet or fleece.

Materials

- 28-in. x 32-in. piece of natural linen (see page 7)
- 28 in. x 32 in. piece of blue poplin
- 27¼-in. x 31¼-in. piece of cotton batten
- 5 skeins of Ginnie Thompson Flower Thread:
  - royal blue (article 535),
  - rose (article 285),
  - green (article 433),
  - chartreuse (article 439),
  - and turquoise (article 505)
- lead pencil
- erasable textile pencil
- 1 sheet of tracing paper
- ruler
- thread to match the linen
- needles
- pins
- scissors
- sewing machine

See motifs and diagrams, page 132

Embroidery stitch to use: running stitch (see page 158)

Easy

**Time: 3 hours without dying,
5 hours with dying, plus
drying time**

Materials

- 26-in. x 60-in. piece of white
  28-count linen (see page 7)
- 1 wire clothes hanger
- 8 large chrome hooks with rings
- 4 bottles of Pebeo Setacolor
  fabric paint, in pink, chartreuse,
  turquoise, and orange
- 4 packets of fiber-reactive dye,
  such as Procion MX, in pink,
  chartreuse, turquoise, and orange
- 1 tube of puffy paint, such as
  Pebeo or Tulip
- erasable textile pencil
- fine paintbrush
- 1 piece of sturdy cardboard,
  4¾ in. x 16 in.
- thread to match the linen
- needles
- pins
- scissors
- hairdryer
- sewing machine
- iron

**See patterns and motifs,
pages 133–34**

A Hanging Organizer
for Baby

Instructions

The Slipcover

- Transfer the patterns to actual size (see General Techniques, page 156) and
  cut out.

- Fold the linen rectangle into two along the long side and match the fold to the
  line marked on the pattern. Warning: Be sure to fold the material and match it
  to the pattern in such a way as to save room for the remaining pieces. Pin the
  pattern onto the linen and cut out both pieces, leaving the fold uncut. Unfold
  the material and lay flat.

- Hem each of the long sides of the slipcover.

- Place the pattern for the gussets onto the remaining linen, pin, cut out, and
  repeat the operation. Hem all four sides of the two gussets.

- Fold the slipcover in two, right side to right side. Pin the gussets so that the
  fold matches the fold of the slipcover (see diagram for the placement of the
  gussets). Sew the gussets directly to the right side of the slipcover.

- Turn the slipcover inside out. Sew from A to B and from A1 to B1. Turn out,
  then hem each side between B and A1. Slip the hanger into the slipcover
  (see diagram).

- Hang the hanger and paint a pattern of small stars, using fine brushstrokes,
  with the four textile paint colors (see motif). Let dry, then iron to fix the paint.

- Place the cardboard into the bottom of the slipcover.

The Pockets

- Place the pattern for the pockets on the remaining linen, pin, and cut out. Repeat three more times, to finish with four 7¼-in. x 13⅝-in. rectangles. Fold in two, iron the fold, then unfold. Hem the two sides parallel to the fold. Fold in two, right side to right side. Sew the sides of the pockets, then turn right side out.

- Paint the pockets with the four colors, following the manufacturer's directions (see General Techniques, page 156). Allow to dry.

- Photocopy the motifs, cut them out, place them onto the center of the dried pockets, and trace their outlines with a textile pencil. Add a few stars (see motifs). Fill them in generously with puffy paint. Let dry, then heat with the hairdryer to fix the paint.

- Attach the pockets to the slipcover, using two rings for each pocket and two hooks on the slipcover for each pocket.

- You can also use Velcro to make the pockets closable, especially useful if you are planning to take the organizer or one of the pockets out with you.

The table

A Flowery Tablecloth

Easy

Time: 12 hours

Materials

- 1 piece of natural linen cloth (size determined by size of table)

- 6 skeins of DMC Pearl Cotton, in shades of pink (articles 601, 902, and 915) and green (articles 907, 469, and 3346)

- 2 sheets of dressmaker's carbon paper

- 6 sheets, 8½ x 11 in., of tracing paper

- lead pencil

- thread to match the linen

- needles

See motifs, page 135

Embroidery stitches to use: running stitch and French knot (see page 158)

Instructions

- Photocopy the motifs at 400 percent and trace one kind of flower on to each piece of tracing paper.

- Place the carbon paper facedown on the fabric and transfer the flower motifs to the fabric from the tracing paper, by tracing over the lines with a pencil.

- Choosing a color for each flower, embroider the lines with a running stitch, making each stitch ⅜ in. long and leaving a little space (five or six threads of the linen) between stitches. For the flowers, use stitches only ¼ in. long, so you can shape the round edges more smoothly.

- Embroider the French knot (see motifs).

- Hem the tablecloth and wash, if necessary.

You can also make matching napkins with a different flower on each napkin; every guest can easily keep track of his own napkin.

Place Mats

Very easy
Time: 1 hour, 30 minutes

Instructions

- Cut the linen into four rectangles, 14 in. x 20 in. each. Hem the four sides of each rectangle ⅜ in. from the edge.

- Trace the three flowers and the blade of grass (see motifs) and transfer them to the foam board. Cut them out to use as stamps.

- Mix a bit of turquoise and white with a touch of black to make a blue-gray. With the flat brush, coat the smallest flower with paint. Carefully position it on the place mat, paint-side down. Place a bit of cardboard over it and gently roll the whole surface with the rolling pin. Carefully remove the cardboard and flower.

- Using the same process, imprint two blades of grass with the same color. Use a paper towel to clean off the excess paint from the stamps.

- With the green-gold paint, imprint two other blades of grass near the blue blades.

- With the velvet brown paint, imprint the hollowed-out flower around the small blue flower.

- With the velvet brown paint, imprint the large flower on the edge of the place mat. Let dry. Place a sheet of parchment on the place mat (so as not to damage the coated linen) and iron (with the iron set to "cotton") to set the paint.

- Repeat the process with the other place mats, varying the positions and colors of the motifs.

The advantage of coated linen is that it is easy to wipe off with a damp sponge.

Materials

- 20-in. x 56-in. piece of coated linen (see page 7)
- 2 pieces of foam board
- 5 bottles of Pebeo Setacolor fabric paint, in green-gold, turquoise, velvet brown, white, and black
- flat soft-hair brush
- 2 or 3 sheets of thick gray 8½-by-11-in. cardboard
- 1 rolling pin
- paper towels
- parchment paper
- 2 sheets, 8½ x 11 inches, of tracing paper
- lead pencil
- thread to match the linen
- needles
- pins
- scissors
- iron

See motifs, page 136

A bit technical

Time: 8 hours, plus drying time

A Gilded Centerpiece Cloth

Materials

- 40-in. x 40-in. piece of gray linen
- 20-in. x 20-in. piece of double-sided iron-on fusible webbing, such as Steam-a-Seam
- 1 roll of double-faced iron-on hem seal
- 1 sheet, 18 in. x 25⅝ in., of acetate (or tape four 8½ x 11-in. sheets together)
- 1 bottle of Pebéo Setacolor Shimmer textile paint in Ash
- 1 tube of glitter gutta
- tracing paper
- roll of parchment paper
- repositionable spray adhesive (for stencils)
- stenciling brush
- flexible crepe paper tape, such as Flex-Mask
- lead pencil
- pair of scissors
- iron

See patterns, diagrams, and motifs, page 137

Instructions

- Cut four triangles (8 in. on each side) out of the double-sided iron-on fusible webbing.

- Photocopy the corner pattern at 200 percent, cut it out, and place it at the corner of one of the triangles of protective leaf. Cut the fusible webbing along the edge of the motif and repeat three more times, so you have four corners.

- Place one cut-out motif (sticky side down) on each corner of the gray linen square, about ½ in. from the edge (see Figure 1). Iron a few minutes to bond the fusible webbing to the linen. Let cool a little, then remove the paper backing.

- Cut the linen along the contours of the motif, ½ in. away from the fusible webbing. Notch the linen along the curves of the motif and fold the tabs you have just made back onto the fusible webbing (see Figure 2). Press with an iron, using a piece of parchment paper between the centerpiece and the heat of the iron, so that the parchment covers the excess fusible webbing.

- Finish the hem around the centerpiece by folding the cloth back ¾ in. Iron the fold. Slide the iron-on hem seal into the hem and iron on hot to seal it to the fabric.

- Photocopy the motif for the center stencil at 400 percent, place it on the acetate, and cut it out. Spray one side of the cut acetate motif lightly with glue and position it in the center of the centerpiece.

- Shake the bottle of shimmer paint. Paint inside the stencil, using small strokes with the stencil brush (don't overload the brush with paint). Remove the stencil and allow the paint to dry.

- Place the crepe paper tape 1¾ in. from the edge of the centerpiece, following the motif along the corners (the flexible tape allows you to make smooth round edges at the corners). With the stenciling brush, paint the exposed outer edge of the centerpiece outside the tape with the shimmer paint, using short, careful strokes (it is better to paint a number of very thin layers than to overload the brush). Dot the outline of the painted areas ⅜ in. from their edges with the glitter gutta (see pattern). Let dry and then iron to set the paint and the gutta.

You can just as easily cut out the iron-on fusible webbing and use it to apply the motif in velvet, satin, or taffeta to the centerpiece cloth.

A Wedding Invitation

Very easy

Time: 15 minutes

Materials

For each envelope:

- 7¼ in. x 8⅜ in. of natural linen (see page 7)
- 5¼ in. x 8⅜ in. of blue voile

For each card:

- 4⅜-in. x 6¾-in. piece of natural linen (see p.7)
- 1 card, 11 cm x 17 cm, for the wedding information
- a decorative rubber stamp
- fabric ink for rubber stamps
- colored embossing powder for the stamp
- iron
- needles
- pins
- scissors
- notched scissors
- hole punch
- 1 piece of raffia

See pattern, page 138

Instructions

- For the envelope: Photocopy the pattern for the envelope at 400 percent and cut out.
- Pin the pattern to the linen, cut along the pattern, and notch the flap triangle.
- Place the voile rectangle on the linen envelope rectangle. Sew the three sides together and turn inside out.
- Stamp the triangle flap with the stamp ink. Sprinkle the motif with the embossing powder and shake the material to get rid of the excess.
- With the iron held above the fabric, heat the stamped image just enough so that the powder swells, being careful not to burn the cloth.
- For the card: Notch the linen rectangle along all four sides.
- Place the linen on top of the card bearing the wedding information and punch a hole through both pieces.
- Thread a piece of raffia through the hole and make a pretty bow to tie the linen and card together.

By altering the dimensions of the envelope, you can create a cover for a valuable book or an intimate journal. You can also stamp the piece of linen tied to the card.

Very easy

Time: 15 minutes for each sachet and 10 minutes for each cone

Little Sachets for Candied Almonds

Materials

For each sachet:

- 4¾-in. x 2⅜-in. piece of natural linen (see page 7)
- 4¾-in. x 6⅜-in. piece of brightly colored voile
- 12 in. of thin linen string
- 1 small mother-of-pearl button with two holes

For each cone:

- 8-in. x 9¼-in. piece of natural linen (see page 7)
- 12 in. of linen string
- 1 small mother-of-pearl button with two holes
- thread to match the linen
- needles
- pins
- scissors

See pattern, page 138

Instructions

Sachet

- Place the linen and voile rectangles one on top of the other. Sew the three sides together and turn inside out.
- Notch the opening.
- Fill with candied almonds. Close the sachet by wrapping the string around it several times. Thread each end into one hole of the button, then make a knot.

Cone

- Photocopy the pattern at 200 percent and cut out.
- Pin the pattern to the linen and cut out. Roll up the cone and stitch the edges. Turn inside out.
- Fill with candied almonds. Close the cone by wrapping the string around it several times. Thread each end into one of the holes of the button, then tie them into a knot.

You can use tulle instead of voile.

A Menu Frame

Very easy
Time: 1 hour

Instructions

- Cut out a 1⅝-in. x 3¼-in. rectangle from the center of the linen (see Figure 1).

- Remove the back of the wood frame.

- Apply the acrylic glue to the front of the frame. Lay the linen over the frame, centered well, and press it down so that the detail of the molding is still visible.

- Cut the interior corners of the linen ¼ in. at a diagonal (see Figure 2) and the exterior corners at ⅜ in. from the frame; fold each side to the back of the frame. Glue the interior and exterior flaps to the back of the frame (see Figure 3).

- Cut the string into four pieces. With the quick-dry glue, attach each piece to a corner of the frame in an arabesque.

Using the same technique, you can also cover a small piece of furniture with linen.

Materials

- 8-in. x 14-in. piece of linen

- 1 molded wooden frame, 10 in. x 8⅜ in., with an opening of 3⅜ in. x 5 in.

- 60 in. of linen string

- acrylic binding medium, such as Liquitex

- scissors

See diagrams, page 138

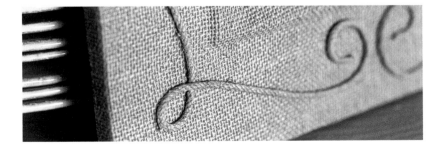

Very easy
Time: 30 minutes

Materials

For each ring:

- 3¼-in. x 7¼-in. piece of natural 28-count linen (see page 7)
- 3¼-in. x 7¼-in. piece of brightly colored voile
- 8 in. of linen string, ⅜ in. thick
- thread to match the linen
- needles
- scissors
- sewing machine

See diagram, page 138

Napkin Rings

Instructions

- Create a hemstitching pattern in the linen by pulling out four adjacent threads at several places along both the long side and the short side (see the diagram for the placement of the gaps).

- Place the linen and voile rectangles on top of each other.

- Place 4 in. of string, knotted at each end, in the center of each short side. Sew three and a half sides. Turn inside out and finish the sewing.

These decorative gaps can ornament linen in other projects (a lampshade or a centerpiece cloth, for example). It is important to use linen with a uniform, regular weave, so that the threads can be easily separated and the gaps will be even.

Tea Time

Instructions

- Photocopy the patterns for the tea-glass holders and the teapot handle and cut them out.

The Tea-Glass Holders

- Fold the linen and match the fold to the area indicated on the pattern for the holders. Warning: Fold the linen and match the pattern in such a way as to leave enough room to cut out all four tea-glass holders and the pattern for the teapot handle. Pin the pattern and cut out both layers of linen, leaving the fold uncut. Repeat steps three more times to end with four tea-glass holders.

- Repeat the steps using the toile.

- Trace a motif onto each of the linen tea-glass holders.

- Sew the beads onto the outline of the motif, using running stitch.

- Place the linen and toile on top of each other, right side to right side. Sew together ¼ in. from the edge, leaving a 2-in. opening. Turn inside out. Slide the cotton wool inside. Sew up the 2-in. opening.

- Finish the tea-glass holders by stitching the short sides together.

Easy

Time: 2 hours, plus 5 hours for the embroidery

Materials

- 8-in. x 24-in. piece of natural 28-count linen (see page 7)
- 8-in. x 24-in. piece of cheesecloth
- 8 in. x 24 in. of cotten batten
- 1 tube of metallic gray glass seed beads
- 4 skeins of DMC embroidery floss:
  - red (article 3685),
  - pink (article 3726),
  - khaki (article 3051), and
  - blue-gray (article 930)
- 1 sheet, 8½ x 11 in., of tracing paper
- lead pencil
- thread to match the linen
- needles
- pins
- scissors
- sewing machine

See patterns, motifs, and diagrams, page 139

Embroidery stitch to use: running stitch (see page 158)

The Teapot Handle Cozy

• Place the pattern onto the remaining piece of linen. Pin, cut out, and repeat the steps to end with two pieces.

• Repeat the steps with the cheesecloth.

• Embroider two pieces of linen with running stitch in alternating colors to make a checkerboard pattern (see diagram). Sew a bead to each cross section.

• Assemble the two embroidered pieces right side to right side. Stitch all around ¼ in. from the edge. Assemble and stitch in the cheesecloth the same way. Stack the linen and cheesecloth. Sew all around ¼ in. from the edge, leaving a 2-in. opening. Turn inside out.

• Slide the cotton wool into the handle. Sew up the opening.

The Tassels

• Cut some 2-in. pieces of embroidery floss, using all six strands. Fold them in two, and tie with one strand of the floss in the same color, leaving enough at the end so it can be sewn to the linen (see diagram). Wind another single strand of the floss around the embroidery thread to finish the tassel. Trim the pieces to equal length, then sew the tassels to the tea-glass holders and to the teapot handle cozy.

To make the project faster, you can also use glitter gutta for the motifs instead of embroidering them.

Materials

- 14-in. x 40-in. piece of natural linen (see page 7)

- 1 old salad shaker

- Mokuba embroidery ribbon, 1 package of each color:
  - ecru (article 470 in 7 mm thickness, and article 558 in 4 mm thickness),
  - orange (article 445 in 4 mm thickness),
  - green (article 340 in 7 mm thickness, article 356 in 7 mm thickness, and article 419 in 4 mm thickness),
  - pink (article 015 in 7 mm thickness).

- 3 skeins of DMC embroidery floss:
  - green (article 987),
  - khaki (article 3051), and
  - ecru (article 3856)

- 1 sheet of tracing paper

- lead pencil

- thread to match the linen

- needles

- pins

- scissors

- sewing machine

- iron

See pattern and motifs, page 140

Embroidery stitches to use: straight stitch, stem stitch, daisy stitch, and French knot (see page 158)

A Salad Shaker

Instructions

The Interior Slipcover

- Photocopy the pattern for the inside of the salad shaker and cut out. Pin the pattern to the linen and cut. Repeat five times. Assemble the six pieces side by side, right side to right side, sewing them on the reverse side, starting from the pointed ends. Turn inside out.

- Cut a 4-in. x 20-in. band of linen. Trace the drawings (see motifs on center of band), keeping in mind that you will hem the band ⅜ in. at the bottom and 1¾ in. at the top.

Embroidery

- Turnips
  With the wide ecru ribbon (article 470), embroider each turnip with a straight stitch.
  With the khaki floss, embroider the rootlets with two straight stitches and the root with two or three small straight stitches.
  With the green cotton, embroider the leaves with four or five straight stitches.

- Carrots
  With the orange ribbon, embroider each carrot with a straight stitch.
  With the green floss, embroider the leaves with a stem stitch.

- Cabbages
  With the narrow ecru ribbon (article 558), embroider the heart with several French knot stitches.
  With the green ribbon (article 340), embroider the leaves with straight stitches all around the heart.

- Peas
  With the wide dark green ribbon (article 356), embroider the pods with two long straight stitches.
  With the wide light green ribbon (article 419), embroider the peas with French knot stitches.
  With the green floss, embroider the leaves with two daisy stitches.

- Radishes
  With the pink ribbon, embroider the radish root with two straight stitches, very close together.
  With the ecru floss, embroider the rootlets with two straight stitches.
  With the green floss, embroider the leaves with two daisy stitches.

- Fold the bottom hem ⅜ in. and sew. Fold the top hem 1⅝ in. with a double fold ¼ in., and iron the fold. Unfold. Place the embroidered band around the opening of the liner, then refold the top hem 1⅝ in. Sew the band to the interior, enclosing the edge of the slipcover. Tack the bottom of the embroidered band discreetly with a few stitches to the shaker liner.

You can also embroider matching napkins or a baby's bib with these vegetable motifs.

Around the House

Somewhat technical
Time: 3 hours

Materials

- 20-in. x 60-in. piece of natural linen (see page 7)
- 20-in. x 60-in. piece of crushed velvet
- 16 in. x 16 in. piece of double-sided iron-on fusible webbing, such as Steam-a-Seam
- 2 pillow inserts, 14 in. x 18 in.
- parchment paper
- 1 sheet of tracing paper
- thread
- needles
- pins
- scissors
- sewing machine
- iron

See motif, page 141

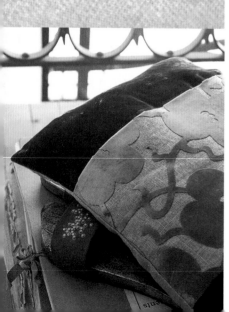

Velvet Cushions

Instructions

- Cut four 8¾-in. x 18¾-in. rectangles and two 8¾-in. x 14¾-in. rectangles out of the linen (for two cushions).

- Cut two 14¾-in. x 18¾-in. rectangles and one 8¾-in. x 14¾-in. rectangle out of the velvet (for two cushions).

- Cut a 8-in. x 14-in. rectangle out of the double-sided iron-on fusible webbing.

- Photocopy the floral motif at 200 percent and trace it onto the paper backing of the fusible webbing.

- Place the 8¾-in. x 14¾-in. velvet rectangle onto the sticky side of the fusible webbing. Iron on hot to heat-seal the velvet and the fusible webbing together. Carefully cut out the motif; you should end up with some leftover pieces of velvet. Place these leftover pieces back onto the pattern and note where they fit, so you can later make a negative of the motif.

- Peel off the paper backing from the floral motif and place it on the 8¾-in. x 14¾-in. linen rectangle. Place the piece of parchment paper on top and iron it to heat-seal the motif to the linen. Fold back ⅜ in. of each long side of the rectangle and pin to the center of the 14¾-in. x 18¾-in. velvet rectangle.

- Fold back ¾ in. of one of the long sides of each of the 8¾-in. x 18¾-in. linen rectangles. Hem the sides.

- Stack two of the linen rectangles you have just hemmed on top of the velvet rectangle with the linen band pinned to it, right side to right side; the two linen rectangles overlap 1⅝ in. Tack the four sides together, then sew ⅜ in. from the edge, leaving a gap at one side. Turn inside out and put the cushion inside.

- With the remaining pieces of the motif, make a second cushion, this time with a negative of the original motif. You will need to arrange the pieces onto the linen so as to re-create the motif in negative.

Crushed velvet can be replaced by raw silk; just remember to contrast the roughness of linen with a more refined and luxurious kind of fabric.

Pleated Bolster

Easy
Time: 3 hours

Instructions

- Cut out two circles, 6 in. in diameter, from the 6-in. x 12-in. rectangle.

- Make a pleat down the center of the long side of the 16-in. x 19¼-in. rectangle, then four more pleats ⅜ in. apart on each side of this center pleat; iron to flatten the pleats.

- Stitch each pleat down ¾ in. from the edge of the fabric. Then, 1⅝ in. down, reverse the direction of the pleats, and again stitch them down (see diagram for the pleats).

- Press down the pleats in the original direction 1⅝ in. farther down, pin them, and again stitch to hold them in place. Continue stitching down the pleats, alternating the direction of the fold, every 1⅝ in. until you reach the other side of the cloth.

- Fold the cloth in two, right side to right side, perpendicular to the pleats. Sew ⅜ in. from the edge to make a cylinder, leaving a 3¼ in. opening in the middle.

- Pin a circle to each end of the cylinder. Sew ⅜ in. from the edges (see diagram for the bolster assembly).

- Turn right side out through the 3¼-in. opening. Stuff with the cotton wool and sew up the opening.

Vary the effect by changing the spacing of the pleats or their size, or by using thread in a contrasting color.

Materials

- 2 rectangles of fine gray linen, 16 in. x 19¼ in.
- cotton wool to fill the bolster
- thread to match the linen
- needles
- pins
- sewing machine
- iron

See diagrams, page 141

Materials

- 18 in. x 28 in. of natural linen (see page 7)
- Cotton wool to fill the cushion
- 1 ball of linen string, about 1 mm thick
- 4 skeins of Ginnie Thompson Flower Thread:
  - dark rose (article 285),
  - bright chartreuse (article 439),
  - bright green (article 505), and
  - turquoise (article 427)
- knitting needles (size 3½)
- thread to match the linen
- needles
- pins
- scissors
- iron

Striped Throw Pillow

Instructions

- Fold the linen in two along the long side. Sew two sides and half of the third together, and turn the cushion inside out.
- Fill with cotton wool and finish sewing the third side.
- Using a jersey stitch, knit a 14-in. x 18-in. rectangle in the following manner: 50 rows of linen thread, 2 rows of green thread, 6 rows of linen thread, 4 rows of rose thread, 4 rows of linen thread, 2 rows of chartreuse thread, 12 rows of linen thread, 8 rows of green thread, 6 rows of linen thread, 4 rows of turquoise thread, and finish with 18 rows of linen thread.
- Iron the knitting with steam, then sew it to the cushion.

Expert knitters can knit the cushion with jacquard motifs.

Somewhat technical

Time: 5 hours

Materials

- 40 in. x 56 in. of brown coated linen (see page 7)
- 12 mother-of-pearl buttons
- 1 ball of brown linen thread or 1 skein of brown embroidery floss
- thread to match the linen
- needles
- pins
- scissors
- sewing machine

See patterns and diagrams, pages 142–43

Slipcover for a Footstool

Instructions

- Transfer the five patterns to actual size (see General Techniques, page 156) and cut out.

- Pin the patterns to the linen and cut out. Cut a circle out of the front following the pattern, notch, fold back the tabs, and sew the hem. Hem the rest of the slipcover according to the directions on the pattern.

- Baste a ¼-in. hem along the four sides of each pocket. Finish sewing the hem at the top sides of the pockets only.

- Pin the pockets to the sides of the slipcover where indicated on the pattern. For the plain pocket, sew on three sides (right, left, bottom) onto the side of the slipcover. For the pencil pocket, sew on three sides (right, left, bottom) to the other side of the slipcover and then sew to make six individual channels (see pattern).

- Assemble, then sew together ⅜ in. from the edge, each of the four sides to the bottom, right side to right side. Then, without turning over, attach the back and two side panels together. Hem the flap before attaching to the slipcover.

- Sew the buttons onto the front of the slipcover (see diagram).

- Make the buttonholes for the two side panels as indicated on the pattern with either the linen or cotton thread.

- Slide the footstool into the slipcover and button it in place.

Change the shape and size of the pockets to adapt this cover to your own needs.

Materials

- 24-in. x 64-in. piece of heavy natural linen (see page 7)
- 1 piece of turquoise leather (about 32 in. across)
- 1 skein of Ginnie Thompson Flower Thread in turquoise (article 505)
- 1 cylinder of high-density foam, 20 in. in diameter and 7⅛ in. high
- 1 disk of thick gray cardboard, 20 in. in diameter
- 40 in. of linen string
- 1 piece of tracing paper
- lead pencil
- thread to match the linen
- needles
- pins
- safety pin
- scissors
- sewing machine
- iron

See patterns and diagrams, pages 144–45

Embroidery stitch to use: running stitch (see page 158)

Moroccan Pouffe

Instructions

- Photocopy the pattern for the top of the pouffe at 140 percent and cut out.

The Circumference of the Pouffe

- Cut out a 12-in. x 64-in. rectangle from the linen. Make a ¾-in. hem along one of the long sides. On the other side iron a ⅜-in. hem, without sewing it.

The Top of the Pouffe

- Pin the pattern for the top of the pouffe to the linen and cut out, following the pattern. Repeat the operation two times, to finish with three linen triangles. In the same way, make three triangles from the leather.

- Trace the pattern for the handle onto the remainder of the leather and cut out. Cut out two 2⅜-in. x 3⅝-in. rectangles from the linen for the handle loops. Fold the loops in three, as indicated in the diagram. Sew a running stitch with the flower thread down the center of the loops, along their whole length.

- Place a leather triangle on top of a linen triangle, right side to right side, and sew them together on one side, ⅜ in. from the edge. Open and place a leather triangle on the linen triangle, right side to right side, and sew this leather triangle to the second side of the linen triangle, ⅜ in. from the edge. Continue in this way, alternating the leather and linen triangles, to make the top of the pouffe (see diagrams).

- Fold back the excess and iron the top to flatten. With the flower thread, topstitch the linen triangles, using a running stitch (see diagram).

- Sew the handle loops to the middle of the large rectangle (the side of the pouffe) as indicated in the diagram, folding each end under ¾ in. Slide the handle into the loops.

- Join the pouffe side piece to the circle of triangles that makes up the top by pinning them together right side to right side, then closing the cylinder by joining the two small sides (see diagram). Baste ⅜ in. from the edge. Sew the baste, and turn inside out. With the flower thread, topstitch the perimeter of the cylinder ⅜ in. from the top, using a running stitch.

- Slide the foam into the cylinder, then insert the cardboard as the base of the pouffe. Using a safety pin, thread the linen string into the ¾-in. hem to make a drawstring channel. Pull on the two ends of string to close the slipcover snugly over the cardboard. Knot the string very tightly.

A bit technical
Time: 30 minutes for the blind,
plus 7 hours for the embroidery

Embroidered Dishcloth Blind

Materials

- 32 in. of natural linen dishcloth fabric with red stripes (sold by the length)
- 1 sheet of dressmaker's carbon paper
- 1 sheet of tracing paper
- 6 skeins of Ginnie Thompson Flower Thread: 3 skeins each of
  - dark forest green (article 454) and
  - bright green (article 427)
- large knitting needle
- upholstery needle with a large eye
- 2 sliding metal cord locks
- 80 in. of thick linen cord (3 or 4 mm thick)
- 1 rod or bamboo stake
- ballpoint pen
- lead pencil
- thread
- needles

See motifs and diagrams, page 146

Embroidery stitches to use: stem stitch and satin stitch (see page 158)

Instructions

- Hem the top and bottom of the dishcloth fabric 2 in. from the edge.

- Photocopy the motif at 200 percent. Place the carbon paper between the linen and the motif on a hard surface. With a ballpoint pen, trace the motif.

- Embroider the leaves using a satin stitch, first with the dark green thread, then making a second line with the bright green thread.

- Embroider the stems, using a stem stitch with dark green thread.

- Cut the cord in two. Thread half of the cord through the upholstery needle and make a knot at the end. Parallel to the red stripes, $5\frac{5}{8}$ in. from the edge of the blind, make a line of large stitches, each about 2 in. from top to bottom. Bring the needle and thread out through the sliding cord lock, then make a knot (see diagram).

- Repeat on the other side, making sure to match the stitches. The visible stitches should be exactly across from the ones on the other side.

- Slide the rod or bamboo stake into the top hem. To raise the blind, all that is needed is to pull the cords through the sliding cord lock.

A length of dishcloth fabric can also be embroidered to make a nice table runner. Together with the window blind, it will make a chic and original matching set.

Souvenir Lamp

Easy
Time: 2 hours, 30 minutes

Instructions

- Cut out a 8-in. x 25⅝-in. rectangle and an 8-in. circle, using the compass or tracing around the lampshade ring, from the linen.

- Cut out a 7⅝-in. x 26⅜-in. rectangle and an 8-in. circle from the acetate.

- In the center of each circle, trace a 2⅜-in. circle and cut it out.

- Print out the photos on transfer paper, cutting off the excess.

- Arrange the transferred images nicely on the linen (face down on the linen). Iron for 1 to 2 minutes to transfer the image. Allow to cool, then peel off the protective film. If you have ironed long enough, this should be easy to peel off; if not, iron again.

The Cylinder

- Pull back the protective film covering the acetate and apply the linen to its sticky side, starting at one of the short sides. The acetate should project ¾ in. beyond the cloth.

- Wrap the acetate around the three-legged frame and close up the cylinder that is created by overlapping the ¾ in. of projecting adhesive acetate.

- Attach the interior of the cylinder to the frame by applying the adhesive border around the frame loop. Place a 8-in. lampshade ring 3 mm from the top of the cylinder and fasten it with the adhesive. Put the socket in the frame.

The Top

- Glue the linen circle onto the acetate circle to make the top of the lamp. Place the other 8-in. ring and the 2⅜-in. ring on the top, on the acetate side, and attach them with the adhesive border. For the 2⅜-in. ring, fold back the border over the edge of the linen.

- Set the top on the cylinder.

If you do not have a color ink-jet printer, there are two other methods: using a two-step transfer system (such as Pebeo's) or taking your photos and linen to a copy store that provides this service (see General Techniques, page 156).

Materials

- **8 in. x 33⅝ in. of natural linen** (see page 7)

- **8 in. x 40 in. of self-adhesive acetate**

- **about 5 vacation photos, digital or scanned (so they can be printed)**

- **1 lampshade frame, 8 in. in diameter, with three legs**

- **2 simple lampshade rings, 8 in. in diameter**

- **1 simple lampshade ring, 2⅜ in. in diameter**

- **1 white border adhesive for lampshade**

- **1 socket and cord set**

- **transfer paper for ink-jet printer**

- **lead pencil**

- **compass (optional)**

- **iron**

Materials

- 20-in. x 56-in. piece of fine ecru linen
- 12-in. x 16-in. piece of natural linen (see page 7)
- 34-in. x 80-in. piece of ecru linen voile
- 20 in. x 80 in. of double-sided iron-on fusible webbing, such as Steam-a-Seam
- 1 sheet of tracing paper
- lead pencil
- thread to match the voile
- needles
- pins
- scissors
- iron

See diagrams and motifs, pages 146–47

Linen Voile Curtain

Instructions

- Cut out a 20-in. x 34-in. rectangle from the linen and another from the iron-on fusible webbing. Note: Cut these out from one corner of the linen, so you will have enough fabric left for the other parts of the curtain.

- Transfer the motif for the bottom border of the curtain at 400 percent onto the paper backing of the fusible webbing. Apply the sticky side of the fusible webbing to the fine linen, and iron on very hot to attach the fabric to the linen. Cut out the motif. Pull back the paper backing and apply motif to the bottom of the voile, with the exposed fusible webbing against the voile. Iron to fasten.

- Apply a piece of fusible webbing, sticky side down, to the natural linen and to the rest of the fine linen. Iron.

- Trace the large leaves (see motifs) onto the paper backing attached to the fine linen, and the smaller flowers to the paper backing attached to the natural linen. Cut out the motifs and peel off the paper backing. Arrange the flowers and the leaves nicely on the voile, spacing them more closely toward the bottom. Iron on very hot to seal the motifs to the curtain.

- Hem the voile on all four sides.

- To make tabs from which to hang the curtain, cut six 2¾-in. x 10-in. rectangles from the rest of the fine linen. Place a 1¼-in. x 10-in. rectangle of fusible webbing in the middle of each rectangle (see diagrams) and fasten to the linen by ironing. Pull back the paper backing. Fold the two large sides of the linen onto the fusible webbing to make 1¼-in. x 10-in. tabs. Iron again to heat-seal the tabs. Fold the tabs in two, fold their edges inward, and sew them on at regular intervals along the top of the curtain.

You can also use cotton voile for this project.

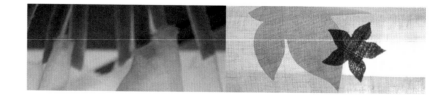

Somewhat technical

Time: 12 hours

Flower Tie-backs

Materials

- 20 in. x 50 in. of natural linen (see page 7)
- 1 m DMC natural linen embroidery ribbon, 3¼ in. wide (length determined by how tightly you wish to tie your drapes)
- 8 in. of green satin ribbon, 1⅜ in. wide
- 1 skein of DMC Pearl Cotton in light beige gray (article 822)
- 1 skein of boutis cotton
- 2 rings, each 1⅝ in. in diameter
- cotton wool
- beige thread
- metallic thread
- large needle for the cotton
- long needle
- scissors
- sewing machine
- iron

See motifs and diagrams, page 148

Instructions

The Corolla

- Photocopy the three sizes of petals, pin them to the linen, and cut out, remembering to leave a ¼-in. border around the edges and at the base of the petals, so they can be sewn together to make the corolla. Repeat this step until you have ten of each kind of petal.
- Place two petals of the same size on top of each other, baste and sew, notch, and turn inside out (see Figure 1). Repeat the step for each of the five petals. Iron the petals so their edges are neat.
- Make a line of ¼-in. stitches in the middle of each petal, to define the rib (see Figure 2).
- Push the boutis cotton, folded in two to give it more thickness, into the rib to give it shape, then cut off the extra cotton (see Figure 3). Insert a piece of wire to stiffen the flower further, and to allow the petal to be shaped.
- With the beige thread, doubled, join the five petals together solidly. Strengthen the flower further with the wire (see Figure 4).

The Center

- Roll the cotton wool into a tight ball about ⅝ in. in diameter.
- Cut a 2⅜-in. circle out of the green satin, sew a loose running stitch around the circle's perimeter, place the cotton wool in the center, and pull the thread together tightly to wrap the satin around the ball (see Figures 5 and 6).
- With a piece of beige Pearl Cotton threaded onto the long needle, run through the center and then back along the outside of the ball to mark off five segments, flattening the ball slightly (see Figure 7). Tightly fasten this ball to the center of a flower. Repeat the step for the other flowers.
- Sew the flowers onto the linen ribbon. Sew a ring to each end.

You can also make the center out of linen, using green embroidery floss. You could make different flowers and attach them all along the linen ribbon, alternating types.

Salvaged Lamp

Easy
Time: 5 hours

Instructions

- Hem one of the long sides of the linen; this will form the bottom edge of the lampshade.

- Make two lines of Maltese tassels, alternating colors. For the first row, make a ¼-in. line for each embroidery point, ¾ in. from the bottom of the linen. Thread a needle with embroidery floss, using all six strands. Push the needle through at the center of the line made by the pencil and pull through, leaving ¾ in. of floss sticking out. Bring the needle back out at the left end of the line, and push it back through again at the far right edge of the line, over the projecting floss. Bring the needle back out in the middle. Trim the excess thread to match the first ¾-in. piece, creating a small tassel. Continue around the circumference of the lampshade, alternating colors. Embroider a second row of tassels 1⅜ in. from the bottom of the linen.

- Attach the long side of the acetate to the bottom of the linen, leaving ⅜ in. of acetate without linen.

- Slide the lampshade frame through the cylinder, against the acetate. Fold the remaining linen into the interior and hem the linen all around the lampshade ring.

- Fit together the shaft and the porcelain base. Fix the socket to the other side of the shaft.

- Slide the electric wire through the base and the shaft, and connect it to the socket. Put in the lightbulb.

Shafts for lamps can be purchased in gold or silver, but you can also paint one.

Materials

- 8 in. x 9¼ in. of natural linen (see page 7)
- 6¾ in. x 9⅝ cm of self-adhesive acetate
- 1 old porcelain lamp fixture (from a flea market)
- 6 skeins of DMC six-strand embroidery floss:
  - khaki (article 935),
  - burgundy (article 3685),
  - mauve (article 3740),
  - olive (article 732),
  - salmon (article 3772), and
  - gray (article 3787)
- 2⅜ in. shaft for the lamp fixture
- 1 electric cord with plug and switch
- 1 socket
- 1 lightbulb
- 1 lampshade frame, 4 in. in diameter
- thread to match the linen
- needles
- sewing machine

Embroidery stitches to use:
Maltese tassel (see page 158)

The Garden

Very easy

Time: 2 hours + 1 hour to dry

Materials

- 36 in. x 46 in. (or as long as you like) of natural linen (see page 7)
- 60 in. of cotton strap
- 1 packet of fiber-reactive dye, such as Procion MX, in dark brown
- 3 bottles of fabric paint, such as Pebeo Setacolor, in turquoise, white, and fawn
- 2 sheets, 8½ x 11 inches, of acetate
- 2 sheets of tracing paper
- stencil brush
- fine brush
- box cutter
- thread
- needles
- pins
- scissors
- sewing machine
- iron

See patterns and motifs, pages 149–150

Garden Apron

Instructions

- Transfer the pattern to actual size (see General Techniques, page 156) and cut out.
- Place the pattern for the apron and the pattern for the pocket on the linen, pin, then cut out. Sew the hems of the apron and the opening of the pocket. Press down the hems around the rest of the pocket with an iron. Position the pocket on the apron, baste, then sew.
- Cut the strap into three pieces of equal length and sew along the lines indicated on the pattern.
- Dye the apron according to the manufacturer's directions (see General Techniques, page 156). Allow to dry.
- Photocopy the flowers and the leaves, once at 140 percent and again at 100 percent, onto the acetate. Cut out, using the box cutter, to create stencils.
- Place the 100 percent flower stencil on the pocket and the 140 percent flower stencil on the bottom left side of the apron (see illustration on page 150), then apply the white paint with the stencil brush. When that has dried well, do the same with the stems and the leaves. Let them dry well, then iron on hot to fix the paint.
- Reposition the stencil over the already-painted flower and apply a coat of turquoise paint. Let dry. Place the other stencil over the already-painted leaves and stems and apply a coat of fawn, mixed with white to obtain a lighter shade. Allow to dry well, then iron on hot to fix the paint.
- Highlight the flowers by hand using the fine brush, using a mix of turquoise darkened with a little dab of fawn. Highlight the leaves with the fawn paint.

When you wear this flowery apron, your garden is sure to thrive!

Somewhat technical
Time: 10 hours, plus about
3 days to dry

Tool Tote

Materials

- 24 in. x 60 in. of very heavy raw linen
- 80 in. of gray-green grosgrain ribbon, 2 in. wide
- 1 polypropylene disk, 8 in. in diameter
- polymer transfer medium, such as Liquitex
- 1 bobbin of heavy-duty beige thread
- 1 bobbin of gray-green thread
- thread to match the linen
- needles
- pins
- scissors
- sewing machine
- iron

See patterns, diagrams, and motifs, pages 151–52

Instructions

- Transfer the patterns for the various parts of the bag (the body is a 12-in. x 26¾-in. rectangle) to actual size (see General Techniques, page 156) and cut out.

- Pin the patterns to the linen and cut out (for the handles of the bag, fold the linen and match the fold to the line marked on the pattern, then unfold it again after cutting).

- Hem one of the long sides of the large rectangle; this will be the top of the bag.

- Color photocopy the tool sketches at 200 percent. Cover the photocopy with a thick layer of transfer medium. Let dry about 12 hours. Soak the photocopy in water, then gently rub it to remove the film from the paper. Only the image should remain on the surface of the transfer medium, which will become transparent upon drying. Allow to dry on a nonporous surface (plastic or ceramic tile, for example). When it is completely dry, coat the back of the image with transfer medium and mount it on one of the pockets with great care (it is very fragile). Allow to dry for 24 hours.

- Hem the top of each pocket as indicated on the pattern. To form the gussets of the pocket, fold back 1¼ in. of each side of the pocket to the back and press down with an iron. Position the right back flap of each pocket along the cylinder, spacing the pockets along the whole length of the cylinder. Pin the folded flap ⅜ in. from the edge and sew onto the cylinder, following the diagram.

- Refold the pocket at the right crease. Stitch down the left side of the pocket ⅜ in. from the edge (you will have to place your hand in the pocket).

- Close the cylinder by placing the back side of each short edge together as shown in the diagram; pin, then sew ¾ in. from the edge. Turn right side out.

- Fit the base of the bag into the bottom of the cylinder; pin, baste ⅜ in. from the edge, then sew the cylinder to the base, also sewing through the bottom edges of the pockets (you will be sewing through three layers between the pockets, and four including the pockets).

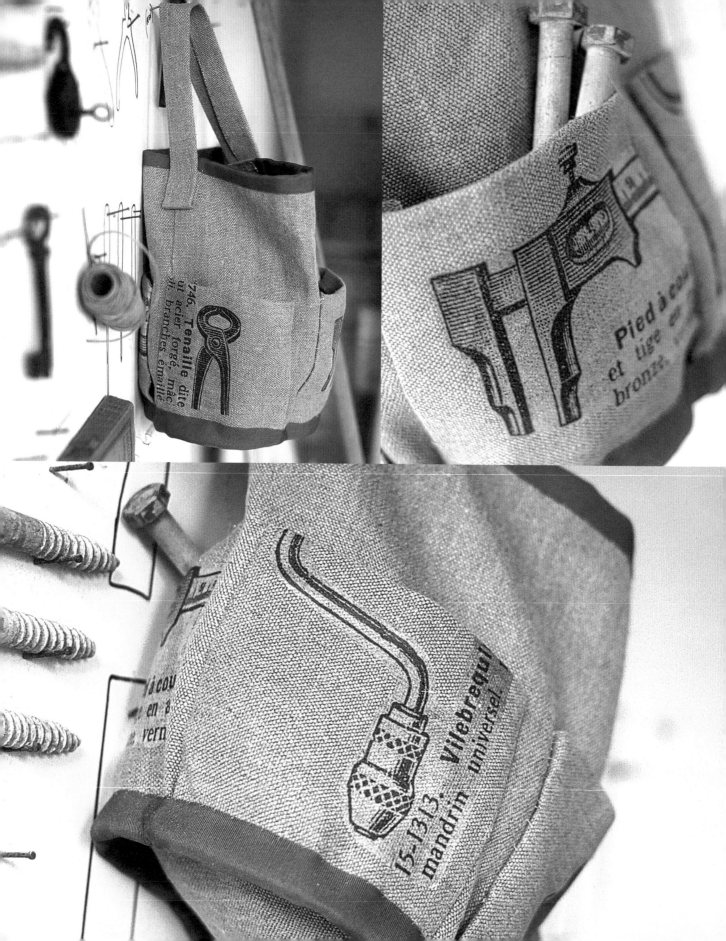

- Fold the right and left sides of the handle under, according to the pattern. Sew these to the back of the handle, following the diagram. Fold the ends of the handle under ⅜ in. Tack the fold down with a few stitches.

- Place the handle on the cylinder; the ends should be opposite from each other, and placed 2 in. from the edge of the cylinder. Sew them onto the cylinder following the diagram.

- Cover the bottom seam with the grosgrain. Pin the edge of the grosgrain 1¼ in. from the edge of the bottom of the bag, fold underneath the bag and pin the other side. Sew both edges of the grosgrain to the bag with the gray-green thread, using small, discreet stitches.

You can avoid the drying time by using a paper transfer (see General Techniques, page 156).

Log Carrier

Easy
Time: 4 hours

Instructions

• Hem the four sides of the raw linen with a double fold so that it will not fray. Lay it out flat.

• Wind the colored linen cord back and forth on top of the linen as shown in Figure 1, pinning it to keep it in place, then stitch it down with six stitches of linen string over each strand of cord at each spot indicated on the diagram (see detail of Figure 1).

• Wrap the cord that projects beyond the linen tightly with more cord, to make the handles. Secure this cord with a few stitches.

• Wrap the natural linen around the polypropylene sheet and fold the edges under on all four sides (see Figure 2). Turn the polypropylene over and place in the center of the log carrier. Sew the natural linen to the rough linen to enclose the polypropylene (see Figure 3).

You can adjust the dimensions of this log carrier for the size of log you most commonly use.

Materials

• 14 in. x 36 in. of very heavy raw linen (see page 7)

• 12 in. x 13¼ in. of natural linen (see page 7)

• 1 sheet of flexible polypropylene (or semi-rigid plastic or cardboard), 10¾ in. x 12 in.

• 33 ft. of colored linen cord

• 33 ft. of natural linen string

• thread

• needles

• upholstery needle with a large eye

• pins

See diagrams, page 153

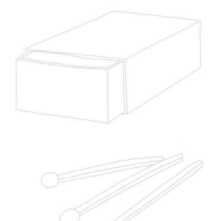

Antiqued Flower Painting

Very easy
Time: 30 minutes, plus about 2 hours to dry

Instructions

- Carefully remove the linen from the frame, using the screwdriver to pry off the nails. Set the nails aside.

- Print the photo onto the transfer paper (see General Techniques, page 156).

- Position the transfer paper, imprinted side down, on the linen removed from the frame. Pass the iron over the reverse of the transfer paper, pressing for a few minutes. Allow to cool, then pull the protective film off.

- Stretch the linen back over the frame, pulling it over the frame edges and tacking it down with the nails at the back of the frame.

- Apply a coat of antiquing varnish and let dry 2 to 3 hours. Apply a coat of the crackle varnish crosswise to that of the antiquing varnish. The first crazing should appear at the end of forty minutes. Allow to dry 24 hours.

- Apply a little black patina with a rag to darken the cracks of the crazing. Wipe off the excess. Allow to dry 24 hours again.

- Nail the hook to the back of the frame.

Any kind of photo can be transformed into a romantic masterpiece . . . an original gift for Mother's Day.

Materials

- 1 prestretched, unprimed natural linen canvas (be sure to ask for unprimed, as otherwise the canvas will be primed with white paint)
- 1 sheet of T-shirt transfer paper
- 1 crackle varnish kit (antiquing varnish and crazing varnish)
- 1 tube of black patina
- 1 rag
- 1 hook for the frame
- 1 flower picture
- stapler
- printer
- paint brush
- screwdriver
- iron

Easy

Time: 3 hours

Materials

- 46 in. x 92 in. of raw linen (see page 7)

- 45¼ in. x 45¼ in. of cotton batten

- 1 tube of squeeze-on white puffy paint (such as Pebeo or Tulip)

- thread to match the linen

- needles

- pins

- sewing machine

- iron

See motif, page 153

Weekend Throw

Instructions

- Photocopy the half-round of crochet design (see motif) at 100 percent and 70 percent.

- Baste a hem ¾ in. from the short edges of the linen rectangle.

- Fold the linen in two, and sew the two opposite sides. Slide the cotton wool into the pouch and sew the final side. Make a few stitches by hand through all of the layers to fasten the cotton wool to the throw.

- Pin one of the half-rounds of crochet design to the throw. With the puffy paint, draw the other half of the motif freehand, matching the photocopy design. When this half is finished, turn the photocopy around and fill in the other half. Continue to draw several crochet motifs of different sizes on the throw.

- Allow to dry and then iron on hot to fix the puffy paint and allow it to rise.

Don't feel you need to be an expert to draw in the motifs; a few irregularities will only add charm. Puffy paint comes in different colors, and the raw linen could be replaced with any other kind of linen.

Quilted Lounge Cushion

Easy

Time: 3 hours, plus drying time for the dye

Instructions

• Cut three 20-in. x 40-in. rectangles out of the linen.

• Dye each rectangle a different green, according to the manufacturer's instructions (you can also use two green dyes, one color for each of two cushions, and then mix the two dyes for the third cushion). Allow to dry.

• Fold each rectangle in two and sew along two and a half sides, ⅜ in. from the edge. Turn the slipcovers inside out.

• Tightly pack each slipcover with the kapok. Finish sewing up the third side.

• Fold in the corners (see diagram) to form the thickness of the cushion. Tack with several discreet stitches to hold the folds in place.

• With the embroidery needle and the DMC Soft Cotton yarn, pad each cushion, following the placements in the diagram. To do this, thread the needle with three strands of the yarn, and push it all the way through the cushion, from front to back, at the spot indicated on the diagram, leaving an inch or so of floss sticking out; bring it back through, ¼ in. from your original hole (see diagram). Make a double knot and trim the two ends of the yarn to the same length. Repeat fifteen times for each cushion, following the placement indicated in the diagram.

• Cut each ribbon into four 12-in. pieces, to end with twelve pieces in all. Sew three pieces to each short side of the cushion that will act as the middle of the mattress (see diagram) and three pieces to one short side of each of the other two cushions. Tie the ribbons together to attach the cushions.

If you make the cushions larger, the mattress could be used as an extra bed.

Materials

• 40 in. x 60 in. of natural linen (see page 7)

• 3 packets of fiber-reactive dye (such as Procion MX) in three shades of green

• 3 skeins of DMC Soft Cotton yarn:
 - turquoise (article 2132),
 - red (article 2346), and
 - chartreuse (article 2142)

• 48 in. of turquoise grosgrain ribbon, ⅜ in. wide

• 48 in. of red grosgrain ribbon ⅜ in. wide

• 48 in. of chartreuse grosgrain ribbon ⅜ in. wide

• 2 large bags of kapok

• 1 kg of coarse salt (for the dying)

• thread to match the linen

• needles

• large embroidery needle with point

• scissors

• sewing machine

See diagrams, page 153

Easy

Time: 1 hour, 30 minutes, plus
15 hours for the embroidery

Materials

- 36 in. x 80 in. of natural linen
  (see page 7) (the dimension can
  be adjusted to fit the chair you
  choose)
- 5 skeins of natural raffia: beige,
  green, blue, red, and white
- glass seed beads: yellows, clear,
  and black for the flower centers
- 2 iridescent beads for the eyes of
  the insect
- 2 sheets of carbon paper for
  cloth
- 1 sheet of tracing paper
- 1 embroidery hoop (optional)
- ballpoint pen
- thread to match the linen
- beige polyester thread
- black thread
- needles
- large raffia needle
- fine needle to attach the beads
- sewing machine
- iron

See diagrams and motifs, pages
154–55

Embroidery stitches used: straight
stitch, stem stitch, daisy stitch,
Boulogne stitch (see page 158)

Embroidered Raffia Chair Slipcover

Instructions

The Slipcover

- Cut out a 18¾-in. x 80-in. rectangle (for the back and the seat) and two
  15¼-in. x 20-in. rectangles (for the sides) from the linen.
- Fold the large rectangle in two 32⅝ in. from the edge. Sew each side of this
  chair back 14 in. from the beginning of the fold.
- Arrange the slipcover pieces as indicated in the diagram. Baste and sew the
  sides of the slipcover to the seat piece. Hem all the edges of the slipcover with
  a double fold. Fold over and iron.

The Embroidery

- Divide the raffia thread, when it is too thick for the job (the stem stitch, for
  example).
- Photocopy the motifs at 100 percent and 200 percent and cut out.
- Place the carbon paper between the cloth and the motifs on a flat surface. With
  a ballpoint pen, trace the motifs. These lines will be covered by the embroidery.
- The ears of wheat
  For the ears: With the beige raffia, embroider with a straight stitch along your
  line. With a very fine piece of thread, make small stitches for the "barbs" at the
  ends of each ear. For the stem: Bring a thread of raffia from the back at the
  bottom of the stem, push the needle back through at the top, and fasten it with
  several Boulogne stitches.
- The daisies
  For the flower: Embroider the petals with a straight stitch, using the white raffia.
  Then fasten the yellow beads to the center. For the stem: Use a stem stitch with
  a thin piece of green raffia.
- The umbels
  For the stems: Embroider using a stem stitch with a thin strand of green raffia.
  For the petals: Embroider using stem stitch with a thick piece of green raffia.
  Fasten a clear bead to the center of each flower.

- **The cornflowers**

  For the flower: Cut a piece of blue raffia into $1\frac{5}{8}$-in. segments; take four pieces at a time and fold in two. Fasten them tightly together with black thread. With the green raffia make the sepals of the cornflower at the base of the petals. For the stem: Embroider using stem stitch with the green raffia. For the leaves: Embroider using straight stitch with the green raffia.

- **The poppies**

  For the flower: With a rather large piece of red raffia, make each petal with a daisy stitch. Fasten the black beads in the center. For the poppy flower bud, embroider using straight stitch with the red raffia, then the sepals with the green raffia following the tracing. For the stems, embroider using stem stitch with green raffia.

- **The grass**

  Cut 2-in. lengths of the beige and green raffia, then fold them in two. Form the small bundles and fasten them to the cloth at the base of the wheat and flowers with a doubled piece of beige polyester thread.

- **The insect**

  For the body, embroider using straight stitch with the green and beige raffia along the motif to form two green triangles and two beige triangles that connect in the center. For the head, embroider using a straight stitch with beige raffia. For the legs, embroider using a straight stitch with a strand of divided raffia. For the antennae, embroider two straight stitches with a strand of very fine thread. Attach iridescent beads for the eyes.

- **The branch**

  With the green raffia, embroider the branch with stem stitch and the leaves with a straight stitch.

For a more understated effect, you could use beige raffia for all of the embroidery.

Patterns, diagrams, and motifs

A Dancer's Wrap Top

$\frac{3}{8}$ in. = $1\frac{5}{8}$ in.

Size 8/10

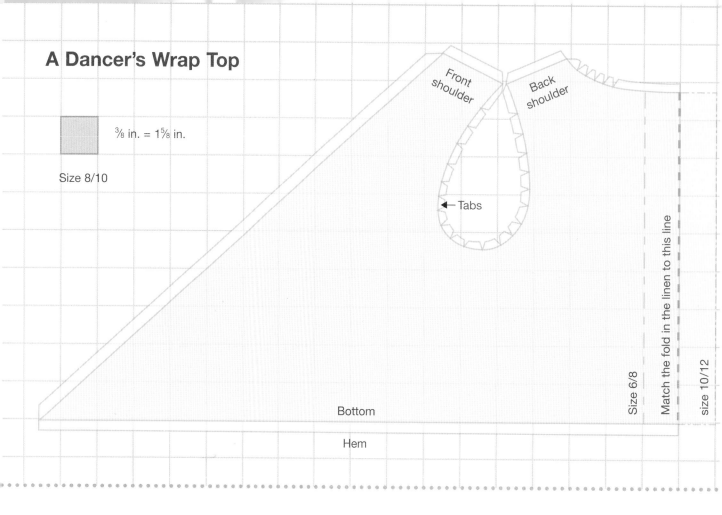

Front shoulder

Back shoulder

←Tabs

Bottom

Hem

Size 6/8

Match the fold in the linen to this line

size 10/12

A Reversible Skirt

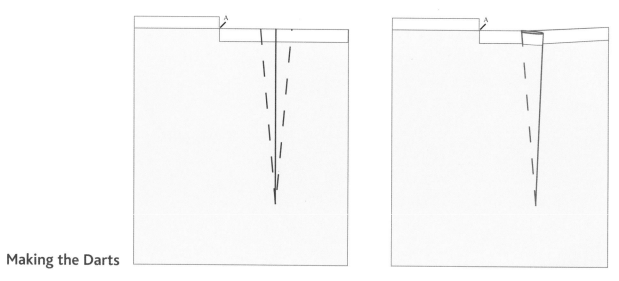

Making the Darts

A

A

A Reversible Skirt

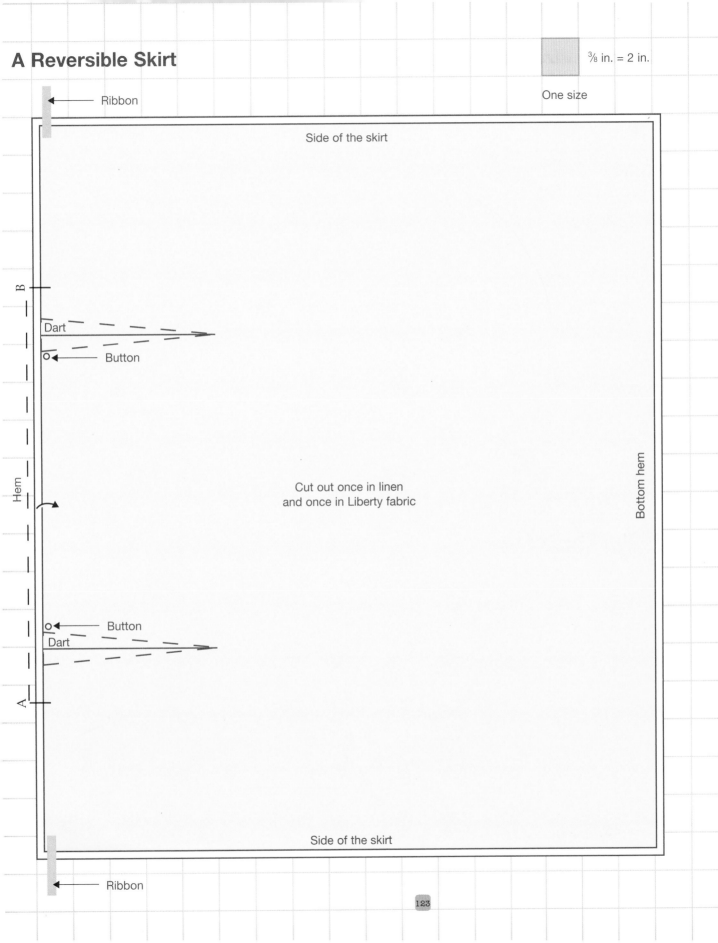

Ribbon

Side of the skirt

B

Dart

Button

Hem

Cut out once in linen
and once in Liberty fabric

Bottom hem

Button

Dart

A

Side of the skirt

Ribbon

A Fringed Tunic

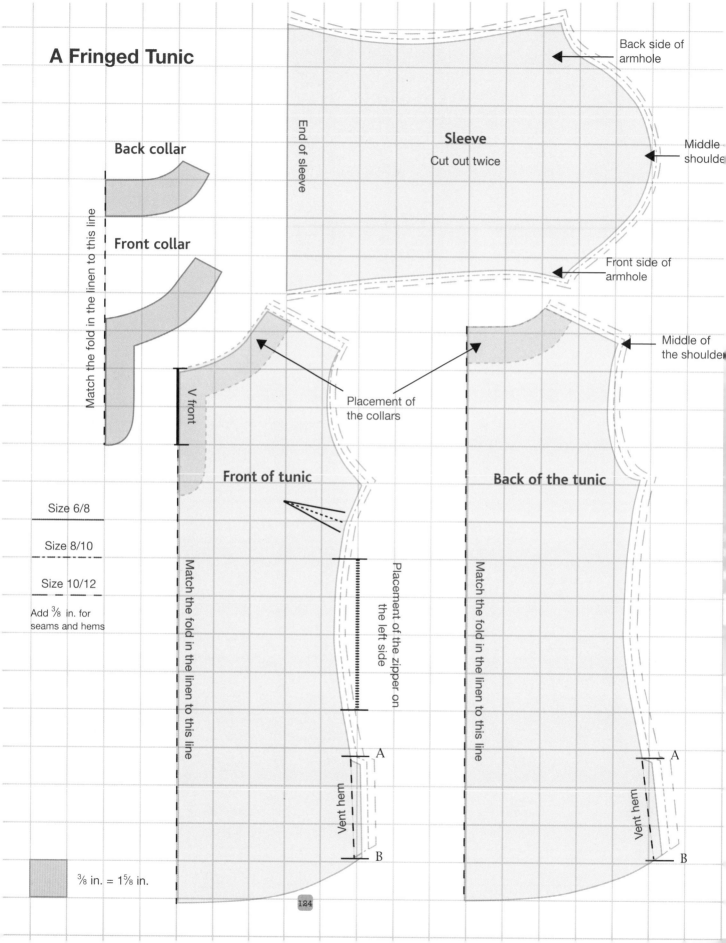

Back collar

Match the fold in the linen to this line

Front collar

End of sleeve

Sleeve
Cut out twice

Back side of armhole

Middle shoulder

Front side of armhole

Middle of the shoulder

V front

Placement of the collars

Size 6/8

Size 8/10

Size 10/12

Add ⅜ in. for seams and hems

Front of tunic

Back of the tunic

Match the fold in the linen to this line

Match the fold in the linen to this line

Placement of the zipper on the left side

A

B

Vent hem

A

B

Vent hem

⅜ in. = 1⅝ in.

An Umbel-Motif Stole

Motifs shown at actual size (100%)

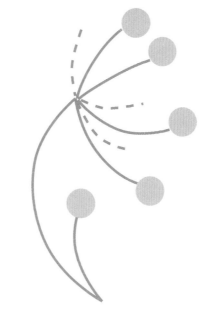

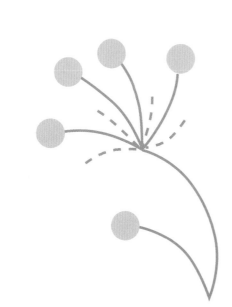

- - - - Glass seed beads

_____ Linen string

Sequins

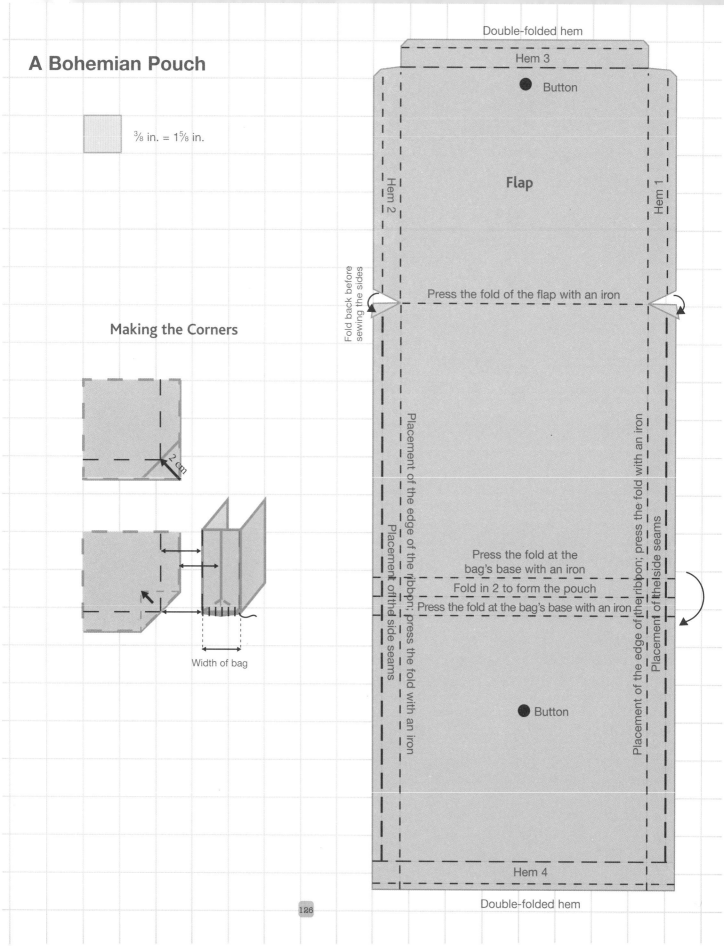

A Bohemian Pouch

⅜ in. = 1⅝ in.

Making the Corners

2 cm

Width of bag

Double-folded hem

Hem 3

● Button

Flap

Hem 2

Hem 1

Fold back before sewing the sides

Press the fold of the flap with an iron

Placement of the edge of the ribbon; press the fold with an iron

Placement of the side seams

Press the fold at the bag's base with an iron

Fold in 2 to form the pouch

Press the fold at the bag's base with an iron

Placement of the edge of the ribbon; press the fold with an iron

Placement of the side seams

● Button

Hem 4

Double-folded hem

A Flower Brooch

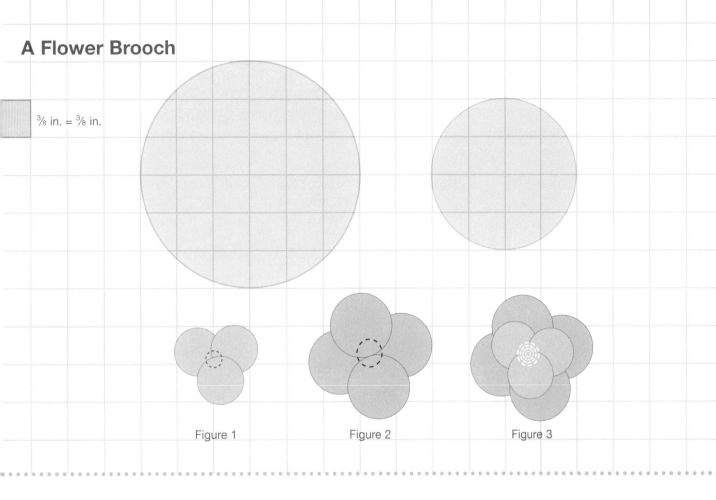

⅜ in. = ⅜ in.

Figure 1

Figure 2

Figure 3

Macramé Bracelets

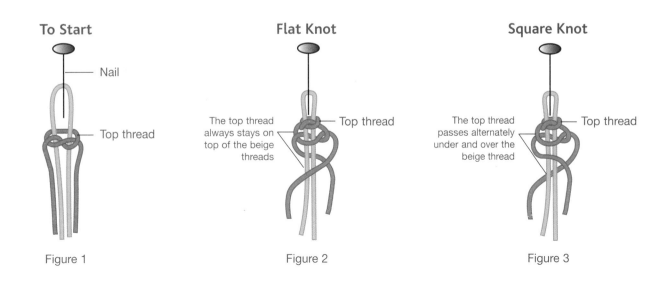

To Start

Nail

Top thread

Figure 1

Flat Knot

The top thread always stays on top of the beige threads

Top thread

Figure 2

Square Knot

The top thread passes alternately under and over the beige thread

Top thread

Figure 3

A Romantic Handbag

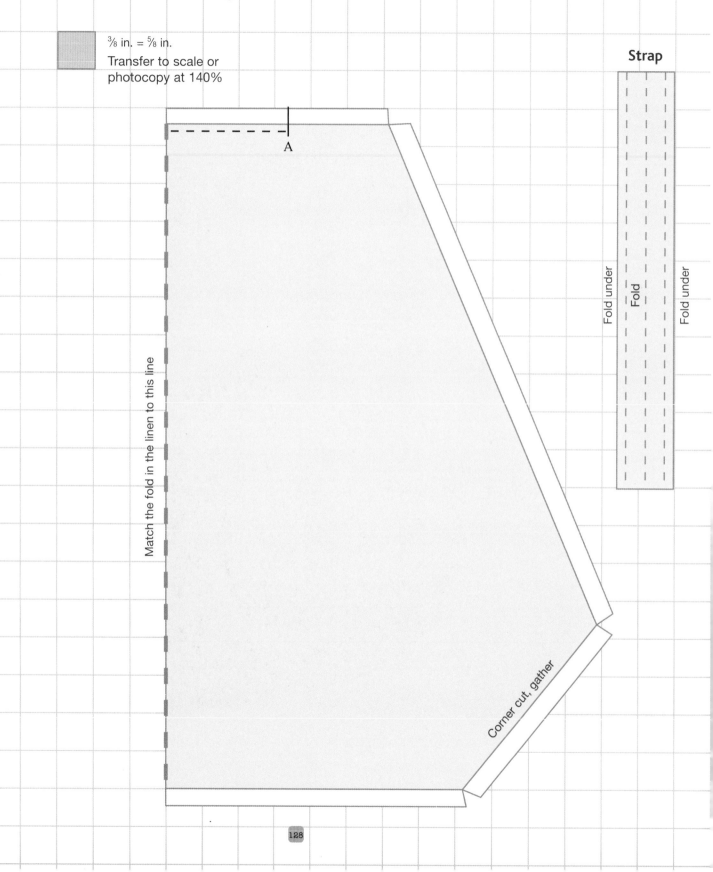

$\frac{3}{8}$ in. = $\frac{5}{8}$ in.

Transfer to scale or photocopy at 140%

Strap

Fold under

Fold

Fold under

A

Match the fold in the linen to this line

Corner cut, gather

A Chicken Tote

Motifs at actual size (100%)

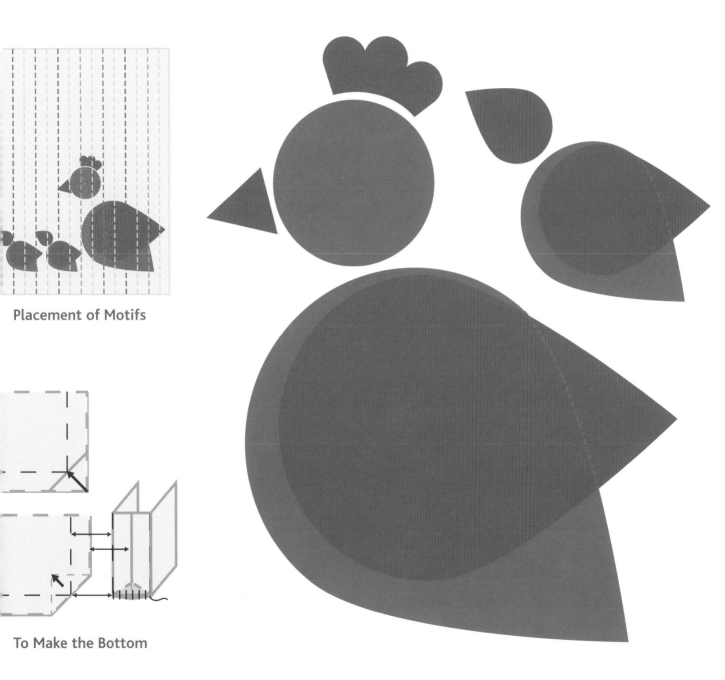

Placement of Motifs

To Make the Bottom

An Elegant Ensemble

⅜ in. = 1⅝ in.

Sides of Hat

Body

Opening to turn inside out through

A

Match the linen and poplin folds to this line

B

Interior side of hat
Cut out once in linen

B

Exterior side of hat
Cut out once in poplin

A

A

C — — D

Sole of Slippers
Cut out 4 times in linen

A   B

C —   — D

Tie

Top of Slippers
Cut out twice in linen
and twice in poplin

Placement
of the snap

Key to Body Sizes

——— 3 months

——— newborn*

— · — 1 month*

- - - - 6 months*

*Add ⅜ in. all around for seams

Key to Slipper and Hat Sizes

········ 6-9 months

——— 3-6 months

— — — 0-3 months

Top of Hat

Cut out 6 times
in linen

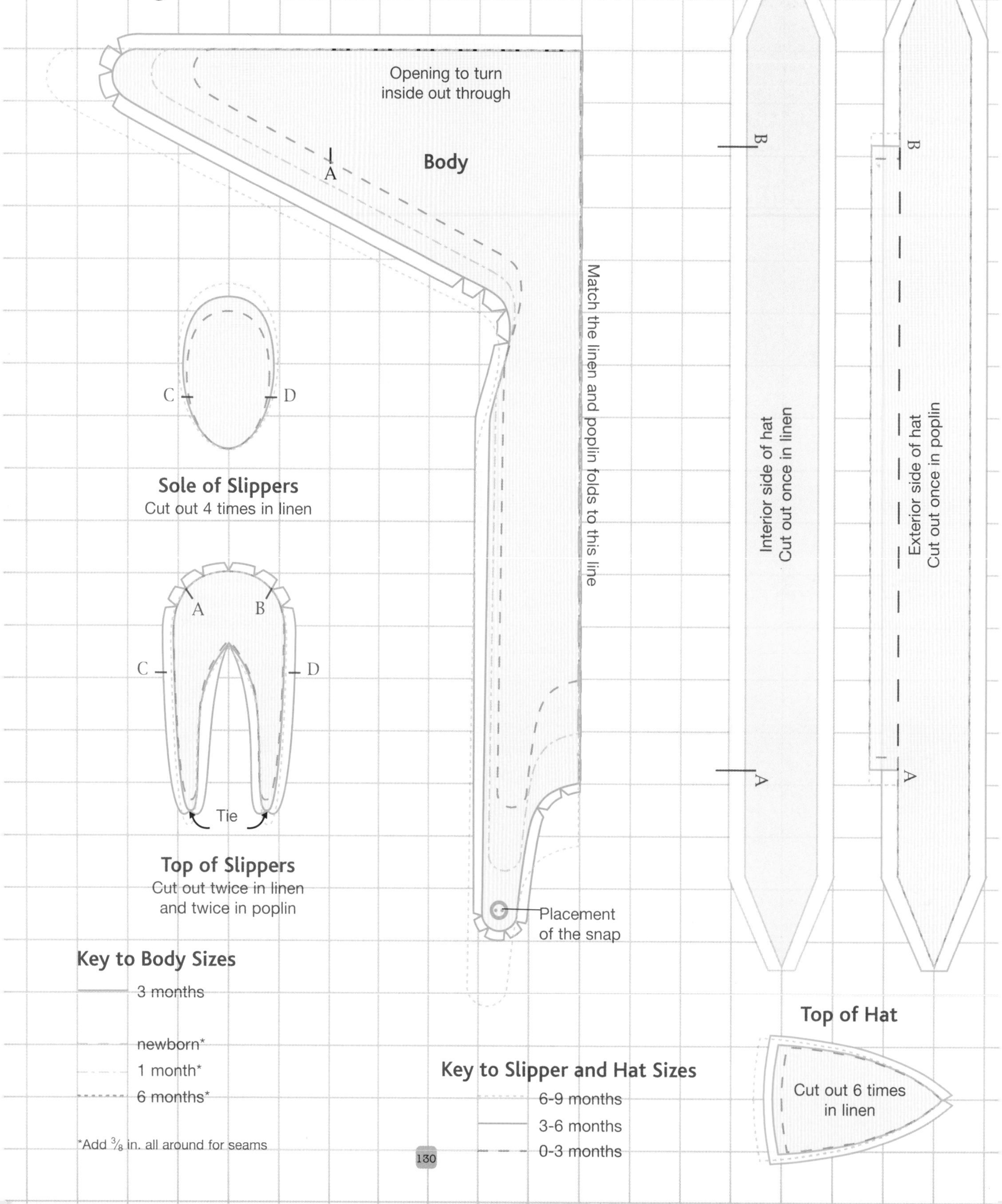

Hat Assembly

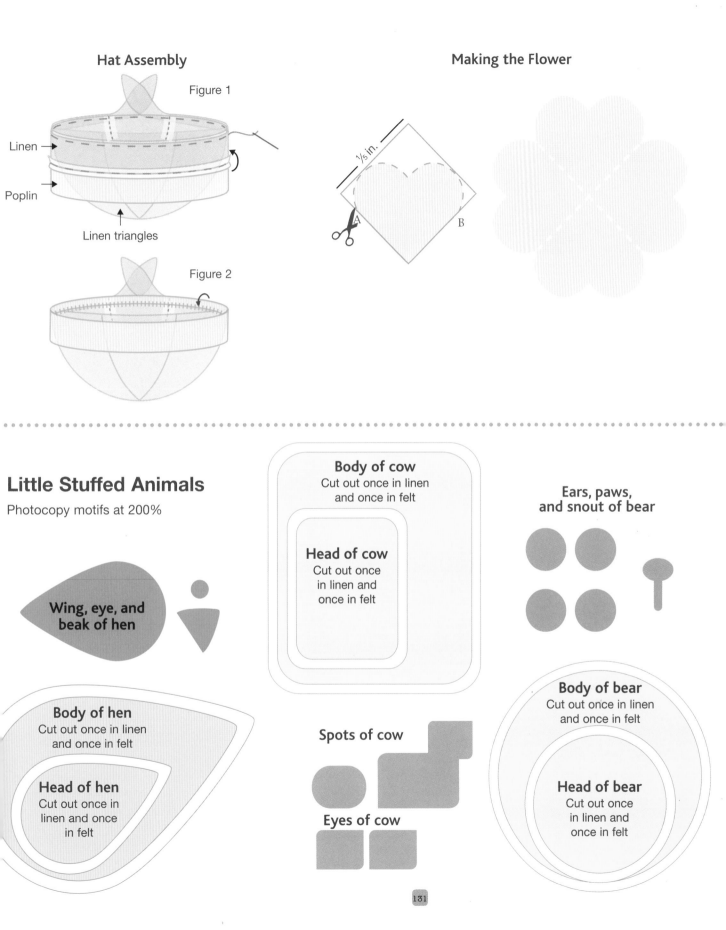

Figure 1

Linen

Poplin

Linen triangles

Figure 2

Making the Flower

⅕ in.

A

B

Little Stuffed Animals

Photocopy motifs at 200%

Wing, eye, and beak of hen

Body of cow
Cut out once in linen and once in felt

Head of cow
Cut out once in linen and once in felt

Ears, paws, and snout of bear

Body of hen
Cut out once in linen and once in felt

Head of hen
Cut out once in linen and once in felt

Spots of cow

Eyes of cow

Body of bear
Cut out once in linen and once in felt

Head of bear
Cut out once in linen and once in felt

A Quilted Baby Blanket

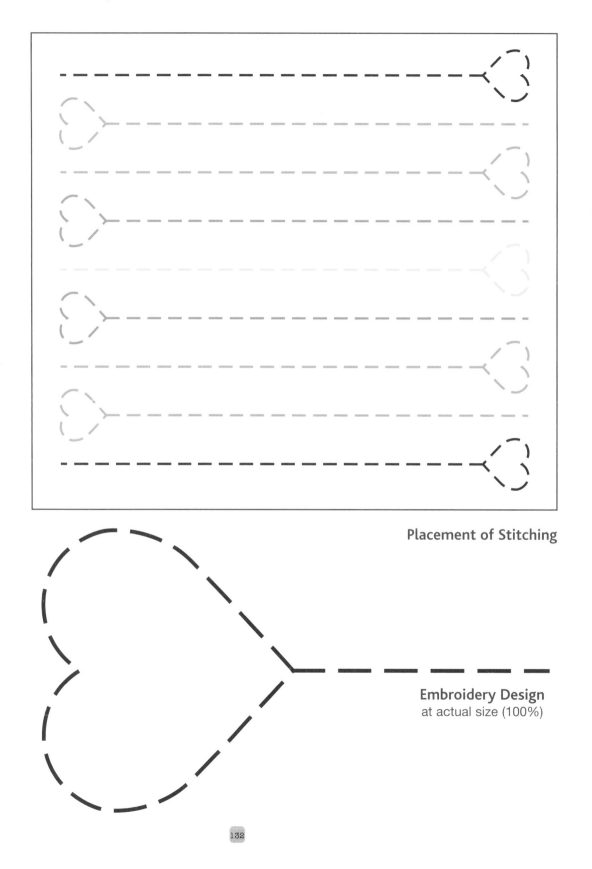

Placement of Stitching

Embroidery Design
at actual size (100%)

A Hanging Organizer for Baby

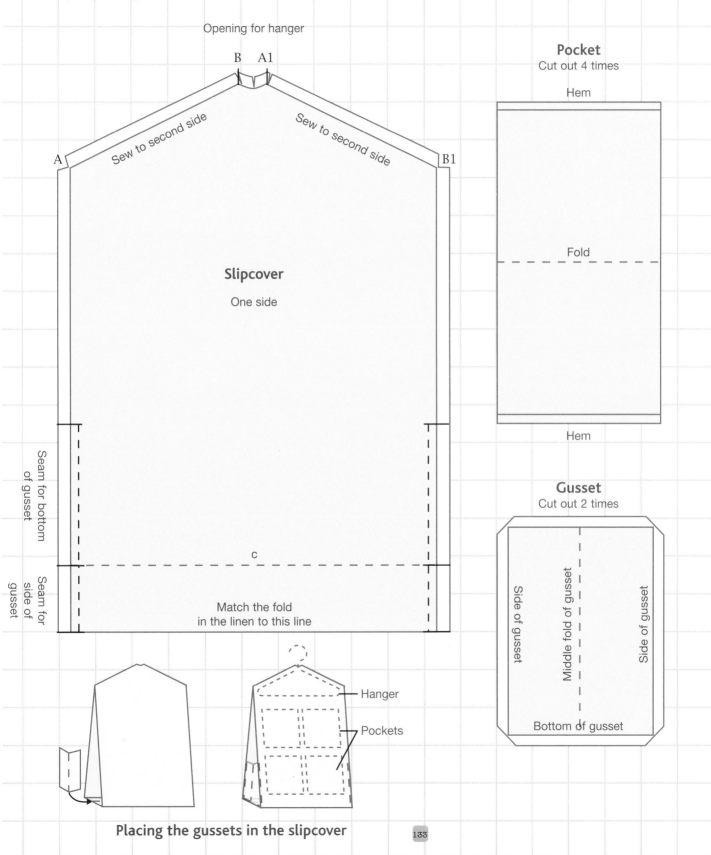

⅜ in. = 1⅝ in.

Opening for hanger

B   A1

A

Sew to second side

Sew to second side

B1

Slipcover

One side

Seam for bottom
of gusset

Seam for
side of
gusset

c

Match the fold
in the linen to this line

Pocket
Cut out 4 times

Hem

Fold

Hem

Gusset
Cut out 2 times

Side of gusset

Middle fold of gusset

Side of gusset

Bottom of gusset

Hanger

Pockets

Placing the gussets in the slipcover

A Hanging Organizer for Baby

Stencil Motifs for the Pockets
at actual size (100%)

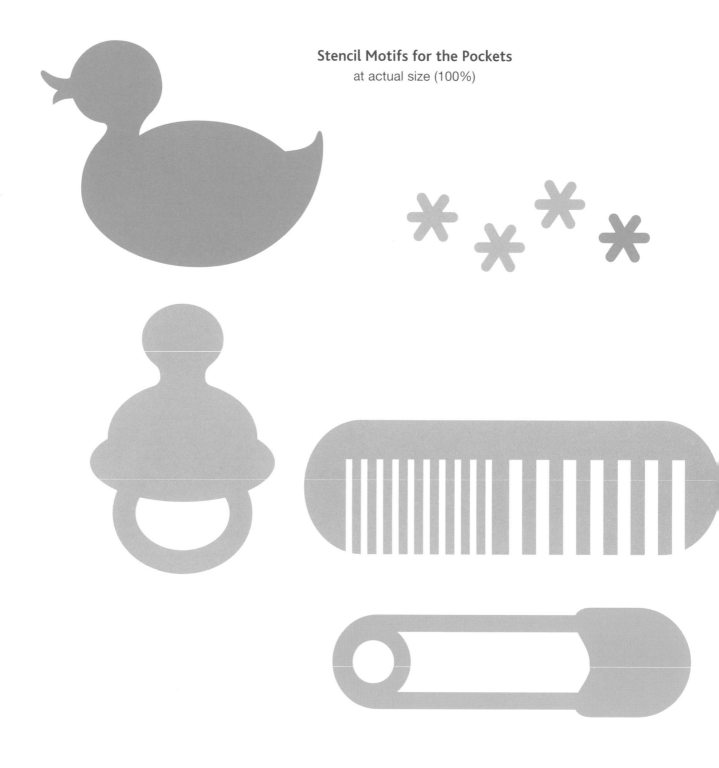

A Flowery Tablecloth

A Flowery Tablecloth

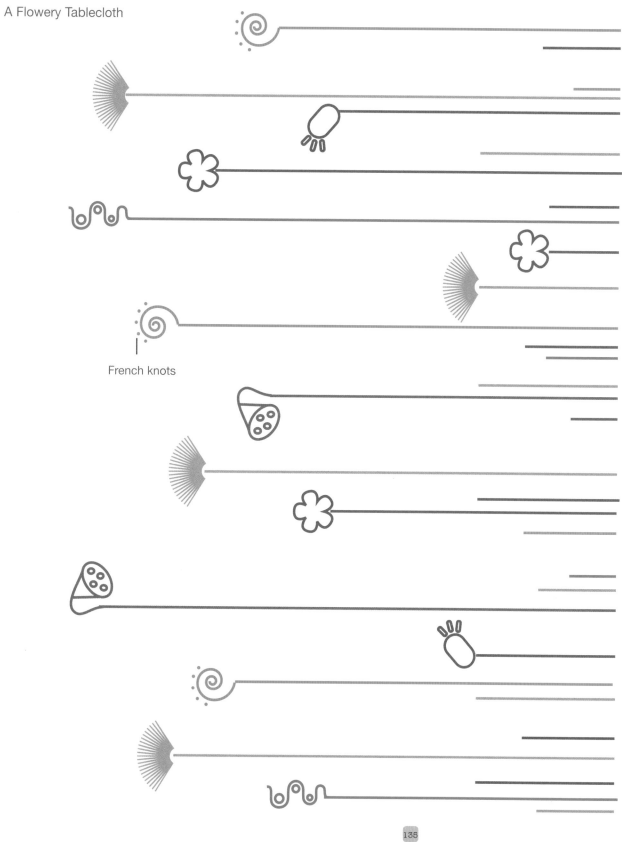

French knots

Place Mats

Motifs shown at actual size (100%)

A Gilded Centerpiece Cloth

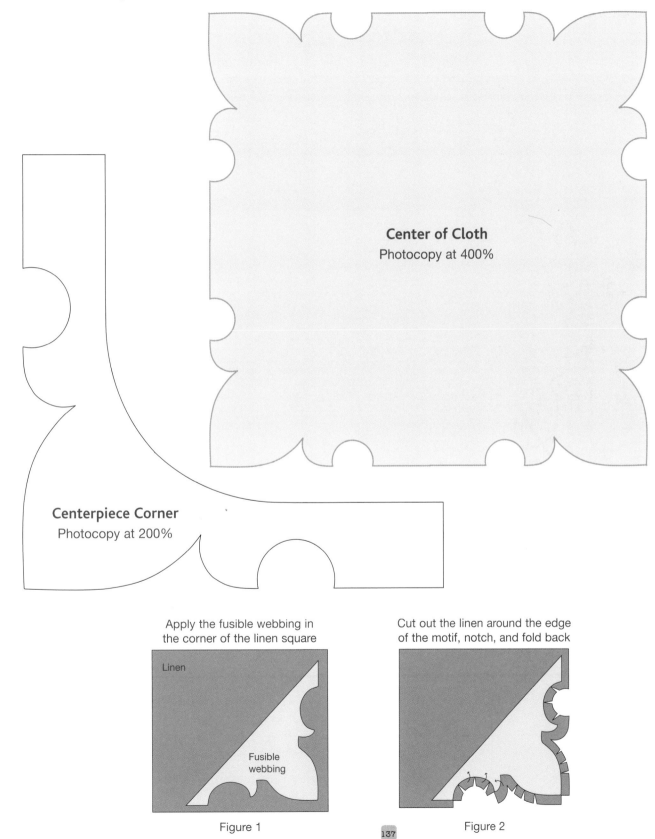

Center of Cloth
Photocopy at 400%

Centerpiece Corner
Photocopy at 200%

Apply the fusible webbing in
the corner of the linen square

Linen

Fusible
webbing

Figure 1

Cut out the linen around the edge
of the motif, notch, and fold back

Figure 2

A Wedding Invitation

photocopy at 400%

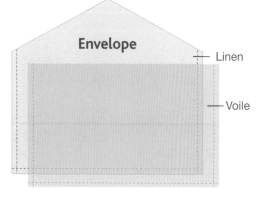

Envelope

— Linen

— Voile

Little Sachets for Candied Almonds

Photocopy at 200%

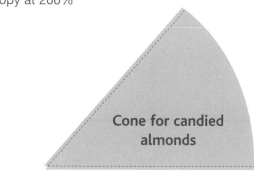

Cone for candied almonds

A Menu Frame

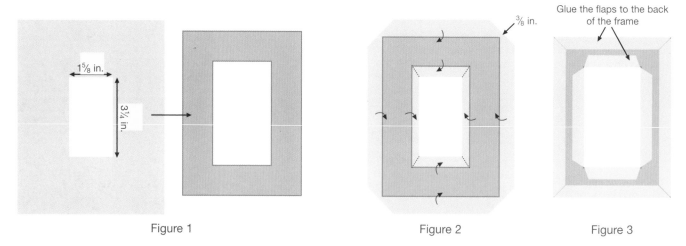

1⅝ in.

3¼ in.

Figure 1

⅜ in.

Glue the flaps to the back of the frame

Figure 2

Figure 3

Napkin Rings

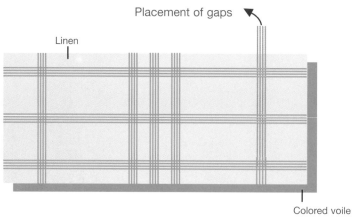

Placement of gaps

Linen

Colored voile

Tea Time

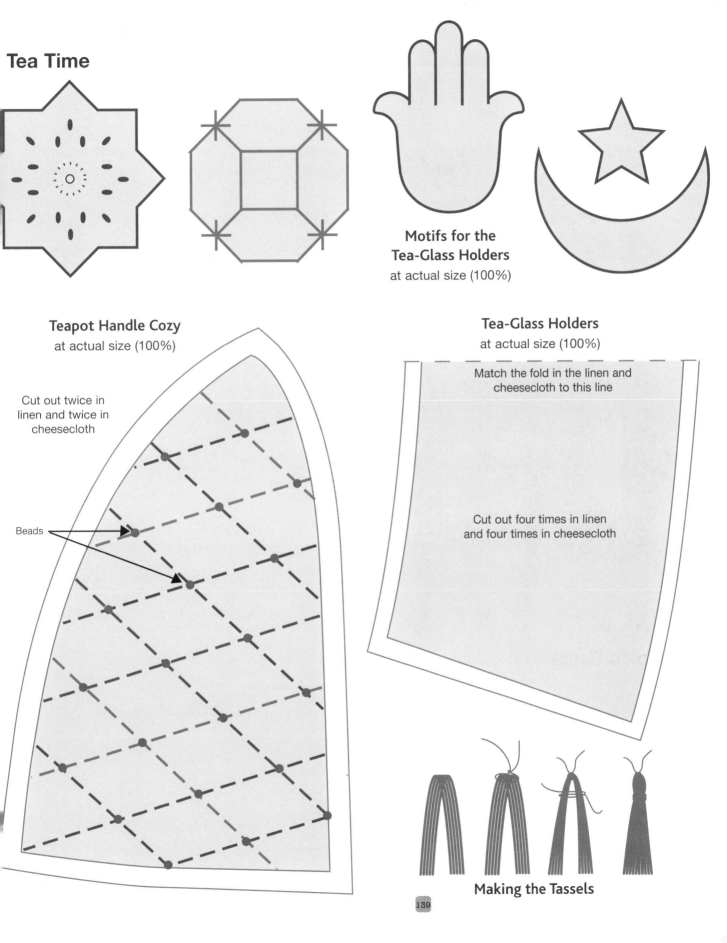

Motifs for the
Tea-Glass Holders
at actual size (100%)

Teapot Handle Cozy
at actual size (100%)

Cut out twice in
linen and twice in
cheesecloth

Beads

Tea-Glass Holders
at actual size (100%)

Match the fold in the linen and
cheesecloth to this line

Cut out four times in linen
and four times in cheesecloth

Making the Tassels

A Salad Shaker

Motifs for the Salad Shaker
at actual size (100%)

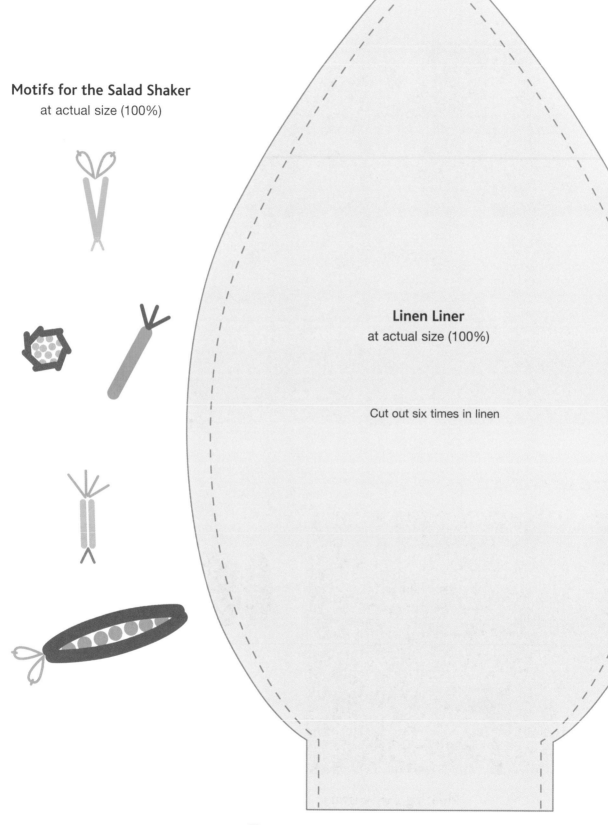

Linen Liner
at actual size (100%)

Cut out six times in linen

Velvet Cushions

Photocopy design at 200%

A Pleated Bolster

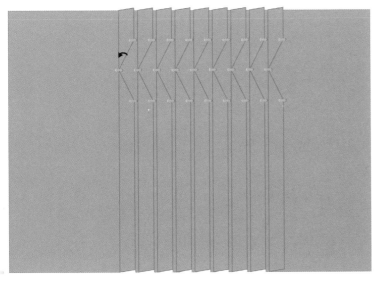

Pleating the Bolster

Bolster Assembly

— Stitches to hold down
the pleats

A Slipcover for a Footstool

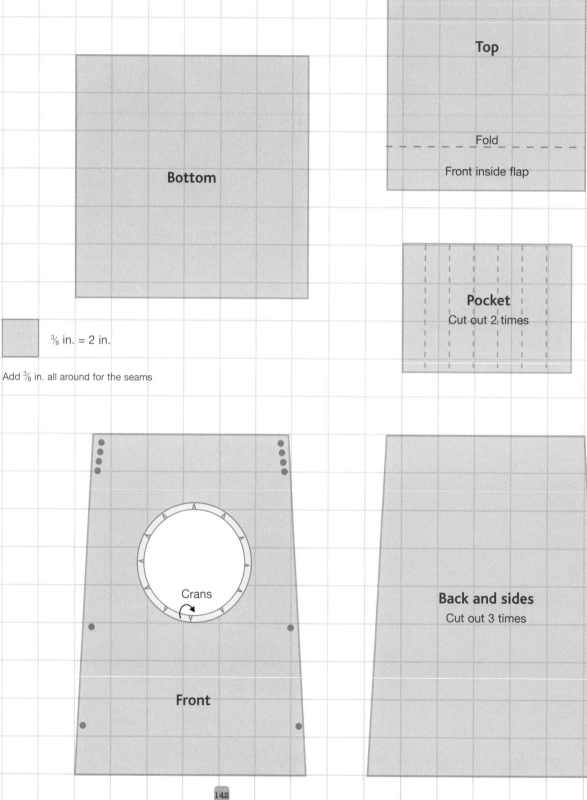

Top

Fold

Front inside flap

Bottom

Pocket
Cut out 2 times

⅜ in. = 2 in.

Add ⅜ in. all around for the seams

Crans

Front

Back and sides
Cut out 3 times

Slipcover Assembly

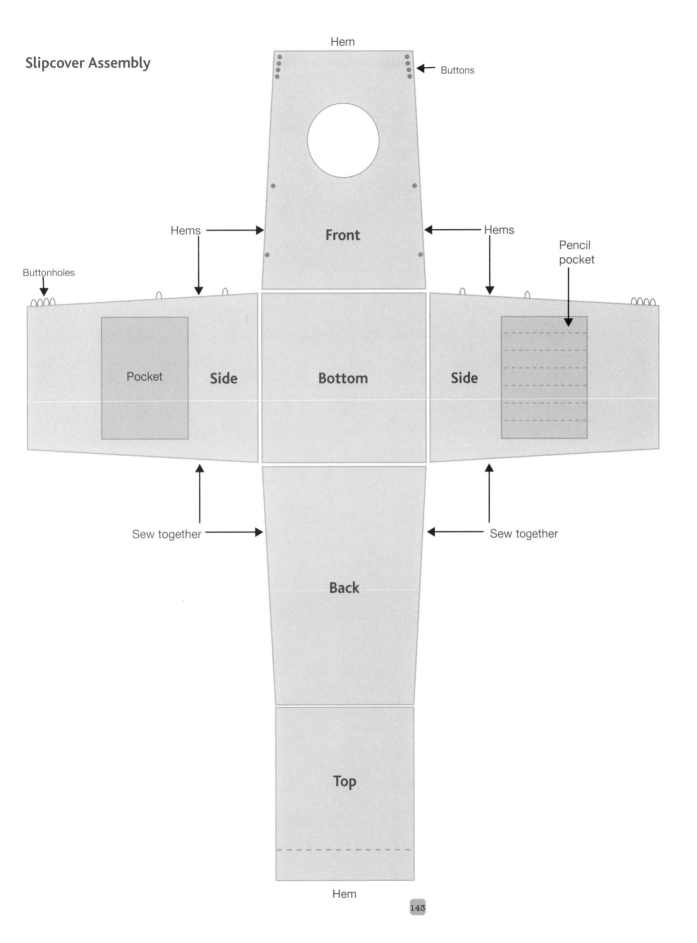

Hem

Buttons

Hems

Hems

Front

Pencil pocket

Buttonholes

Pocket

Side

Bottom

Side

Sew together

Sew together

Back

Top

Hem

143

A Moroccan Pouffe

Photocopy at 140%

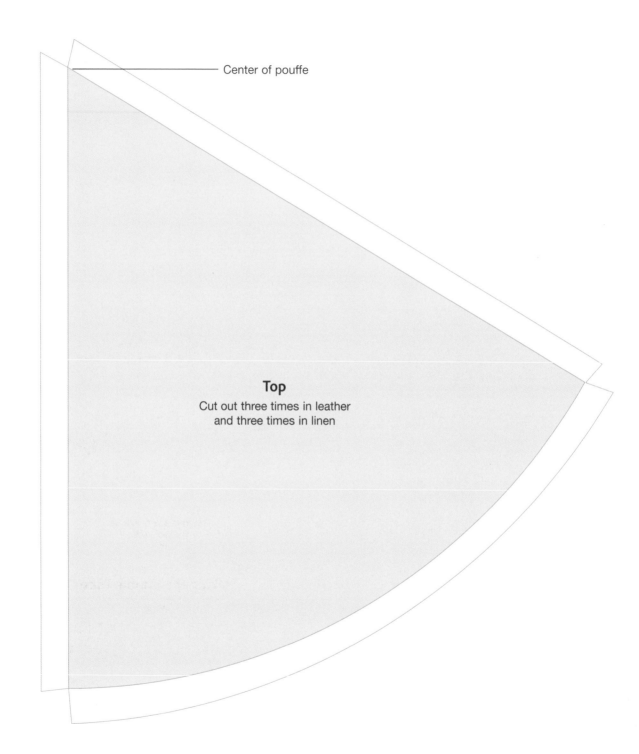

Center of pouffe

Top
Cut out three times in leather
and three times in linen

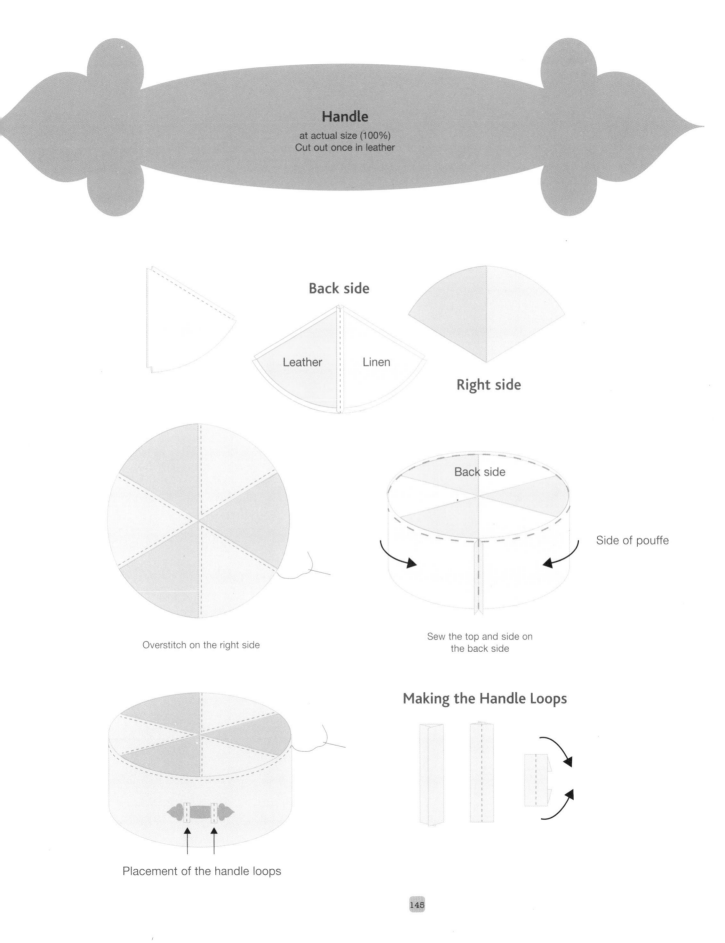

Handle
at actual size (100%)
Cut out once in leather

Back side

Leather Linen

Right side

Overstitch on the right side

Back side

Side of pouffe

Sew the top and side on
the back side

Making the Handle Loops

Placement of the handle loops

An Embroidered Dishcloth Blind

Photocopy the motif at 200%

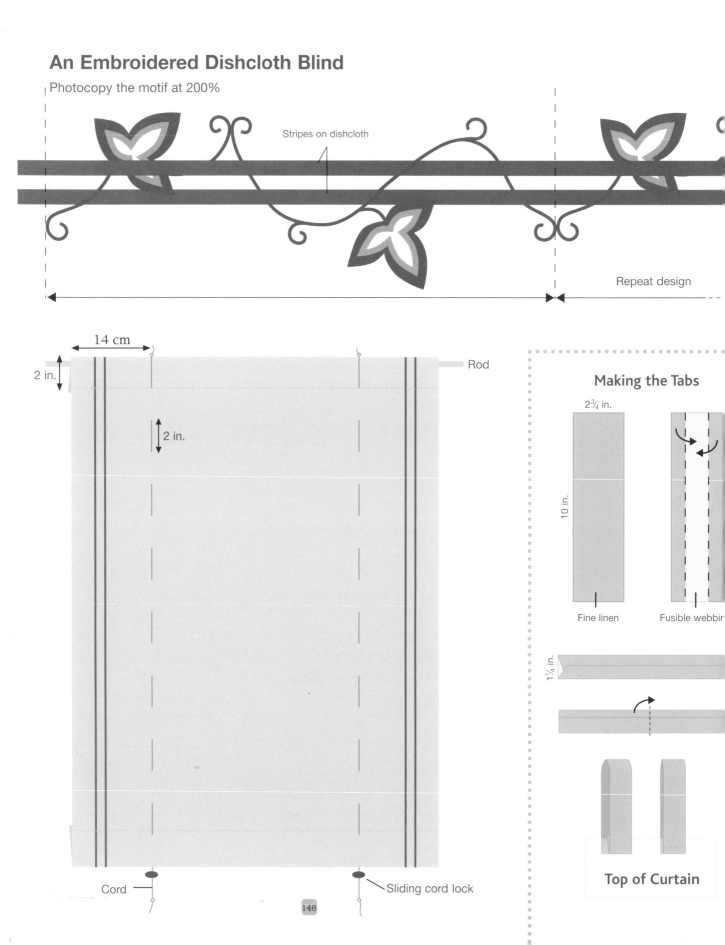

Stripes on dishcloth

Repeat design

14 cm

2 in.

2 in.

Rod

Making the Tabs

2¾ in.

10 in.

Fine linen

Fusible webbir

1¼ in.

Top of Curtain

Cord

Sliding cord lock

A Linen Voile Curtain

Motifs at actual size (100%)

Bottom of Curtain

Photocopy the design at 400%

Flower Tiebacks

at actual size (100%)

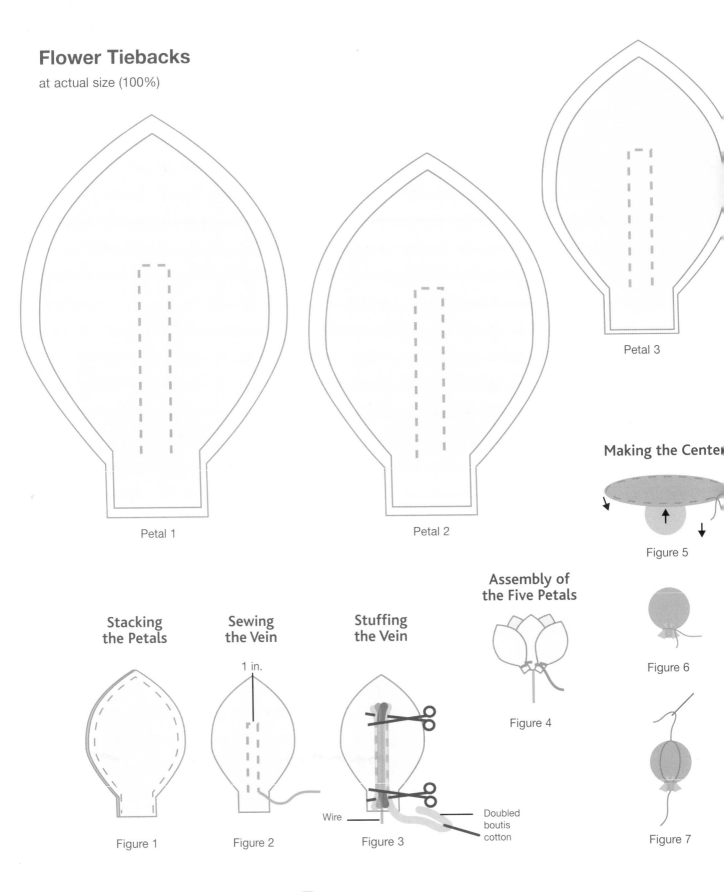

Petal 1

Petal 2

Petal 3

Making the Center

Figure 5

Figure 6

Figure 7

Assembly of the Five Petals

Figure 4

Stacking the Petals

Figure 1

Sewing the Vein

1 in.

Figure 2

Stuffing the Vein

Wire

Doubled boutis cotton

Figure 3

A Garden Apron

$\frac{3}{8}$ in. = 2 in.

Strap

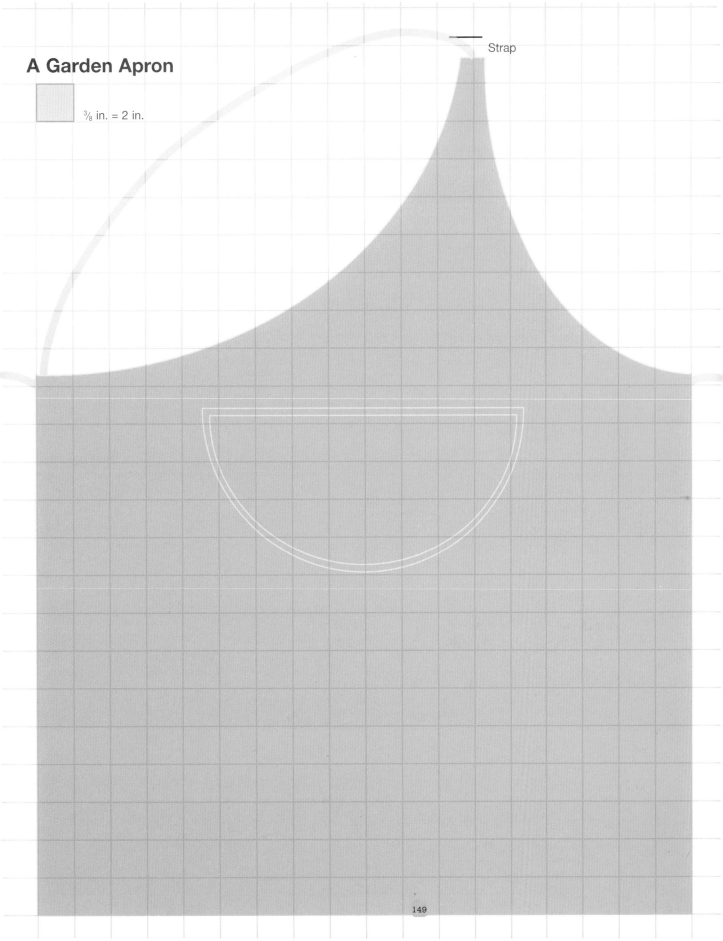

A Garden Apron

Photocopy the motif at 100% and at 140%

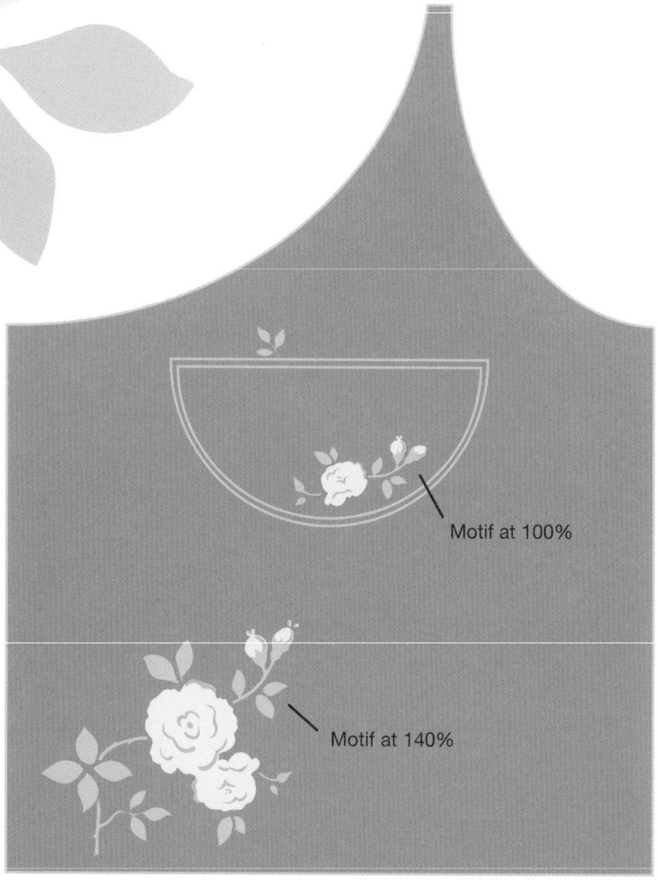

Motif at 100%

Motif at 140%

A Tool Tote

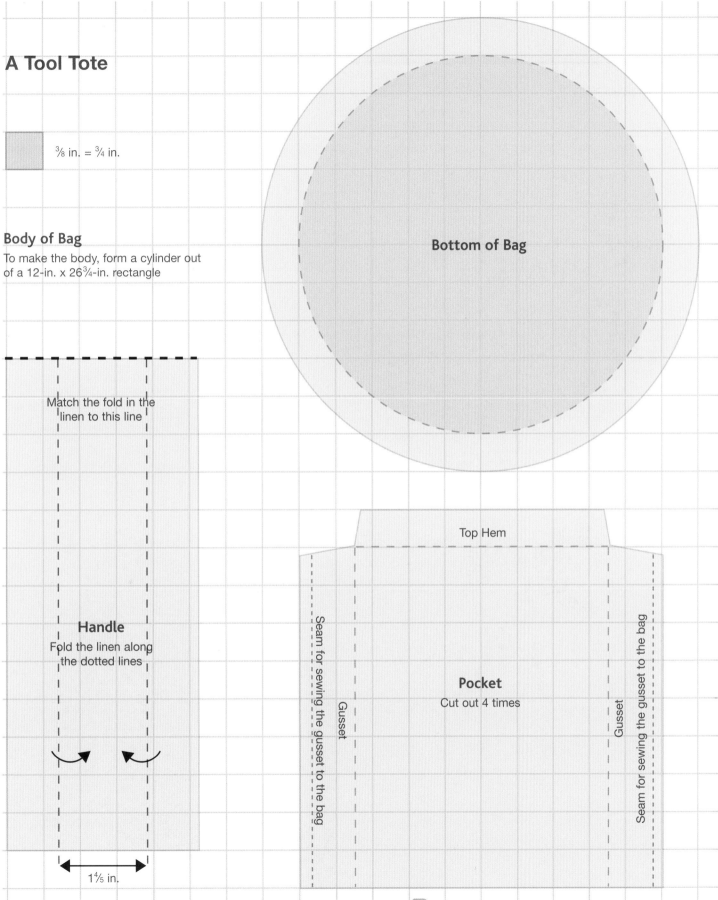

⅜ in. = ¾ in.

Body of Bag
To make the body, form a cylinder out of a 12-in. x 26¾-in. rectangle

Bottom of Bag

Match the fold in the linen to this line

Handle
Fold the linen along the dotted lines

1⅘ in.

Top Hem

Seam for sewing the gusset to the bag

Gusset

Pocket
Cut out 4 times

Gusset

Seam for sewing the gusset to the bag

A Tool Tote

Photocopy the images at 200%

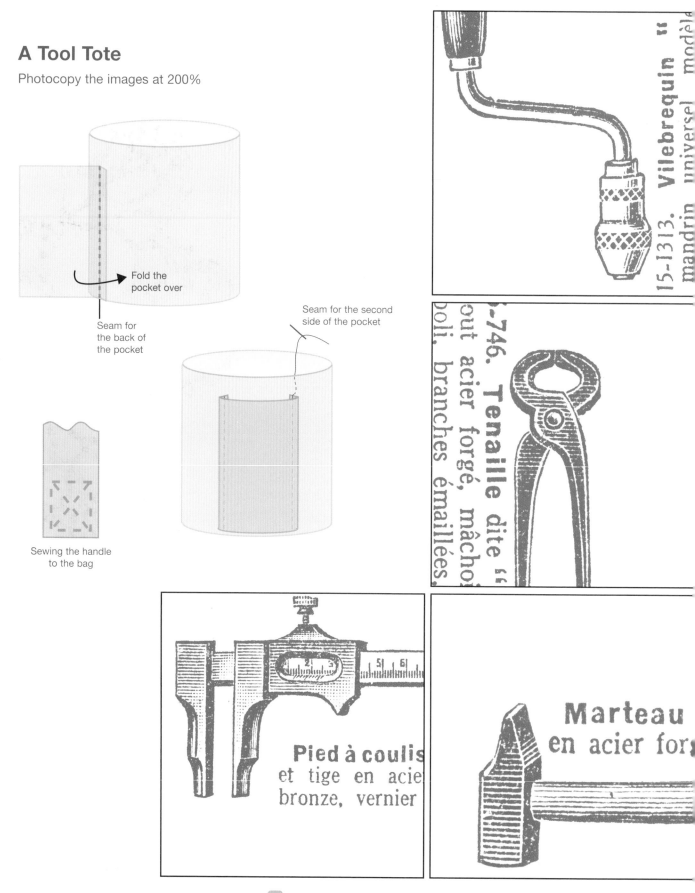

Fold the pocket over

Seam for the back of the pocket

Seam for the second side of the pocket

Sewing the handle to the bag

15-1313. **Vilebrequin "** mandrin universel modèl

746. **Tenaille** dite ͏ out acier forgé, mâcho oli, branches émaillées.

Pied à coulis et tige en acie bronze, vernier

Marteau en acier for

A Log Carrier

Outside of Carrier

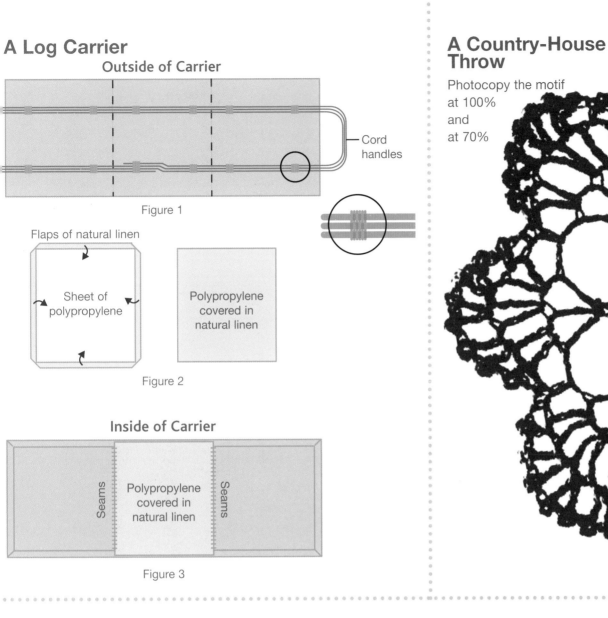

Figure 1

Cord handles

Flaps of natural linen

Sheet of polypropylene

Polypropylene covered in natural linen

Figure 2

Inside of Carrier

Seams

Polypropylene covered in natural linen

Seams

Figure 3

A Country-House Throw

Photocopy the motif
at 100%
and
at 70%

A Quilted Lounge Cushion

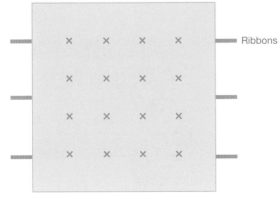

Ribbons

Placement of the quilting stitches and the ribbons on the middle cushion

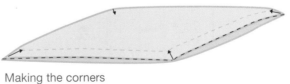

Making the corners

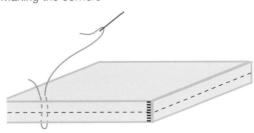

Quilting the cushions

A Raffia-Embroidered Chair Slipcover

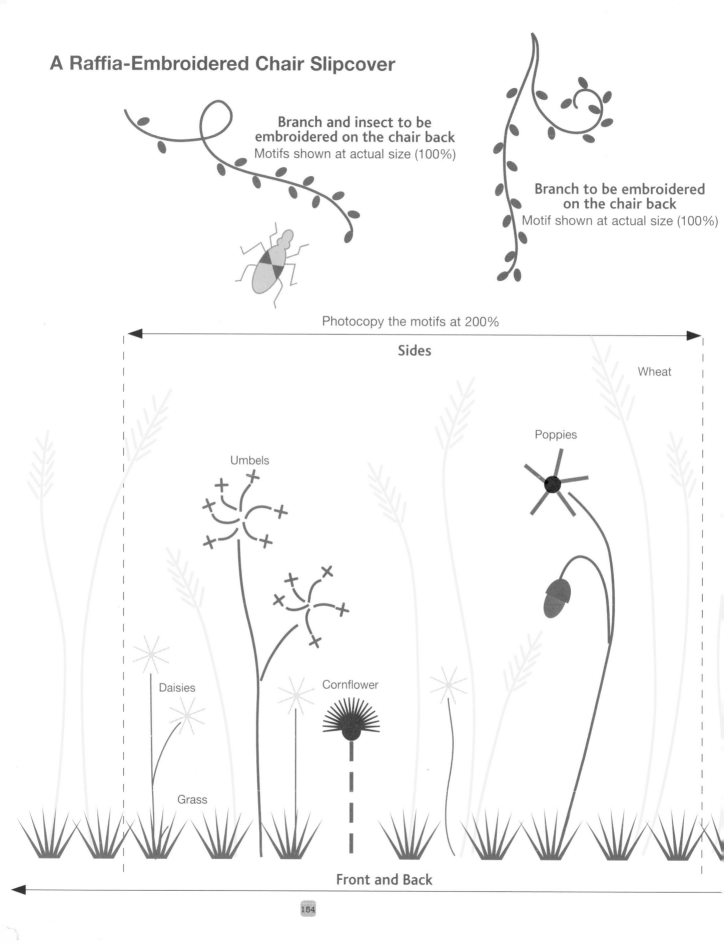

Branch and insect to be embroidered on the chair back
Motifs shown at actual size (100%)

Branch to be embroidered on the chair back
Motif shown at actual size (100%)

Photocopy the motifs at 200%

Sides

Wheat

Poppies

Umbels

Daisies

Cornflower

Grass

Front and Back

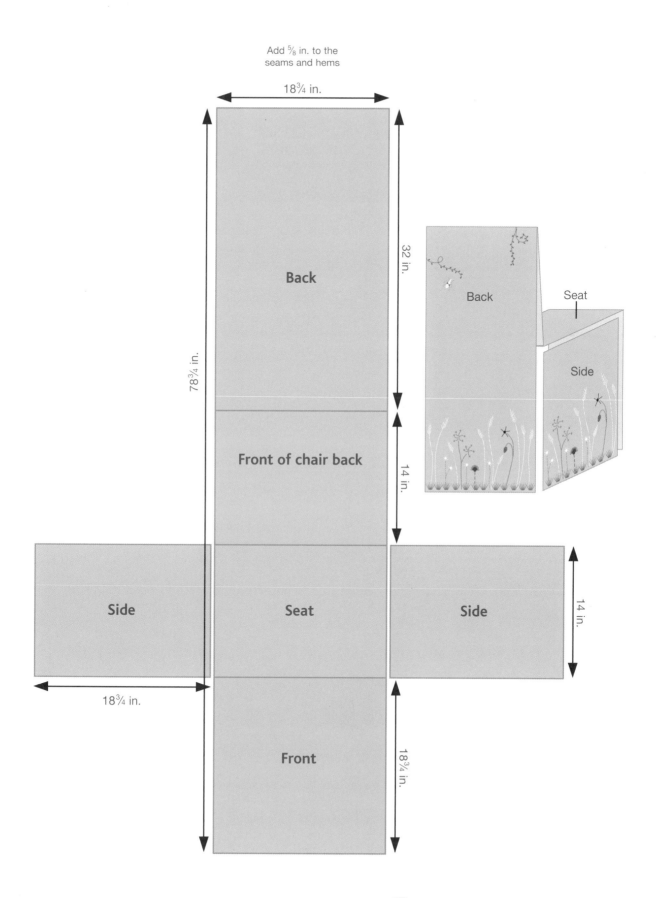

Add ⅝ in. to the
seams and hems

18¾ in.

Back

Front of chair back

Side

Seat

Side

Front

32 in.

14 in.

78¾ in.

18¾ in.

14 in.

18¾ in.

Back

Seat

Side

General Techniques and Necessary Tools

The projects in this book are very simple to make; you don't need to be a great seamstress or a pro at patterns. Here are the main techniques that you will need to know. They are all very easy to master, with often amazing results.

• Transferring a Pattern on a Grid to Actual Size

Draw a large grid onto a piece of craft paper following the directions on the pattern (for example, if the pattern indicates $\frac{3}{8}$ in. = 4 in., then make the lines of the grid 4 in. apart). Reproduce the pattern on the new larger grid. Each square of the pattern will equal that of one of the new large grid.

Cut out the pattern.

• Dying

There are many different kinds of dyes to choose from, depending on the quality of the cloth you are using and how much dyeing you will be doing. Linen is a natural fabric that is quite resistant to dyeing, so you must use fiber-reactive dyes in hot water, either by hand or in the washing machine.

For small dye jobs, you can dissolve the packet of dye in a pot of hot water with some coarse salt. It will take about twenty minutes to obtain the final tint.

For larger dye jobs, a washing machine is more practical. Wash the fabric with the dye once at 140°F, then wash it for another cycle at 190°F.

In all cases, follow the directions on the dye package.

Procion MX fiber-reactive dyes are available from Dharma Trading Company, among other suppliers, in a very large choice of colors, with seasonal additions. You can also mix two colors; though the results can be unpredictable, this is a useful way to create varied shades of one color (see, for example, the quilted lounge cushion on page 113).

• Fabric Paint

You can find fabric paint in a number of stores. These can be opaque, transparent, or even metallic, like those found in the Setacolor line from Pebeo. These paints are very easy to use; applied with a paintbrush, they are then fixed by ironing. Twenty-four hours after the paint has been fixed, you can wash the painted cloth at 100°F.

Fabric paints can create a wide range of effects: a raised "embroidered" look, opalescent colors, a taffeta finish, and metallic shades of gold and silver.

Always wash fabric before painting it, to ensure that the paint adheres well.

All the Setacolor paints come in small bottles. Certain colors are also available in pens, so you can outline your design more precisely, or write words on fabric.

• Fabric Paints in Tubes

Some fabric paints come in paste form in a tube with a pointed tip that allows for precise drawing. Because of their texture, the resulting design is in high relief. These are perfect for outlines, but not for filling in large areas.

Among the paints available in tubes are:

– *Puffy paint* (Pebeo and Tulip are two commonly available brands). This paint puffs up when exposed to heat from an iron or hot plate. It can give an effect like embroidery (see, for example, the country-house throw on page 110).

– *Gutta*. Originally on silk, to outline motifs that would later be painted in, with linen, it is used by itself to create designs. Numerous colors are available in craft stores, with various effects—iridescent, mother-of-pearl, glitter . . .

• Transfer Techniques

There are two ways to make transfer prints:

– With a computer and a color printer. A number of brands of transfer paper are available in 8½ x 11 format. Made for T-shirts, these transfers work well with other types of fabric, especially linen:

Choose a photo or a drawing. Scan it if it is not already in digital format. Print it onto the transfer sheet on the side indicated by the manufacturer. Cut out the motif if it does not take up the entire sheet. Position it on the fabric, printed side toward the cloth. Place a protective sheet (usually supplied by the manufacturer) between the cloth and the iron. If you do not have a protective sheet, you can use a piece of parchment paper. Make sure that the transfer has cooled completely before you peel back the protective sheet.

The printed cloth should be washed inside out on a wool cycle. If you iron the fabric, always protect the transfer with a piece of parchment paper.

– If you don't have a computer or a color printer, you can use the transfer kits sold in craft shops. The process is simple but time-consuming:

Make a color photocopy of the image you want to transfer. (This is essential; you cannot use an original or a page from a magazine.) Coat the photocopy with a thick layer of the medium. Allow to dry overnight to create a plastic film. If the layer is not thick enough, begin again. Immerse the photocopy in a basin of water to soften the paper, and then rub it, removing the paper so that you are left with only the image on the plastic coating.

Coat the exposed image with another layer of medium and place it on the fabric, wet medium against the cloth. Press firmly to remove any bubbles. Allow to dry.

The fabric should be washed in cold water, and care should be taken not to abrade the image. The image will at first seem to disappear, since the medium whitens in water (as in its original state), but when the fabric dries the image will reappear. These transfers are very shiny.

—Another alternative: More and more copy centers offer transfer service. All you have to do is bring them your drawing or photo and your fabric.

• Rubber Stamps

Rubber stamps, used with special fabric ink, allow you to imprint not only designs but also words and initials on your fabric. These inks should be fixed by ironing.

Fabric ink can be combined with embossing powder that expands when heated, giving your design a higher relief. This powder is applied to the stamp print while the ink is still wet. Shake the excess powder off, and then heat the print to inflate the powder. The most practical is a special heat gun, which provides intense heat but doesn't have a fan like a hair dryer. Otherwise an iron or a kitchen hot plate will work fine.

• Double-Sided Iron-On Fusible Webbing

This fabric comes under various brand names, with slight differences. It is covered by a translucent paper backing on which you can trace your motifs. Some brands that are easy to find at fabric stores or craft shops are Steam-a-Seam, Therm-O-Seal, and Heat-n-Bond.

To use: Trace the motif onto the protective film.

—Heat-seal the fusible webbing onto the cloth you will use for the motifs (the unprotected side against the cloth) with an iron (use the hottest setting possible for the cloth you are using).

—Cut out the motifs.

—Peel back the paper backing.

—Position the motifs onto the cloth that you are decorating (unprotected side to the cloth) and iron, on the hottest setting possible for the fabric you are using.

This fusible webbing is very thin, so it does not add any bulk. You can use it to join together two kinds of fabric (as in the romantic handbag on page 30 and the velvet cushions on page 76) or to bind hems without sewing.

• Acrylic Binding Medium

This white acrylic medium comes in jars; it can painted onto cloth to stiffen it or varnish it (for example, see the flower brooch on page 25). One easily found brand is Liquitex.

• Fillers and Stuffings

—Cotton batten. Purchased by the yard in various widths, it is used as a quilting filler in projects like the country-house throw on page 110 and the chicken tote on page 35.

—Synthetic cotton wool. Bought by the bag, it can be used to stuff most objects, large or small (see the pleated bolster on page 79 and the stuffed animals on page 40). It is very easy to use, as it does not fall apart, and it is very soft.

—Kapok. A natural material for the stuffing of certain cushions, kapok is a little more difficult to use, as it tends to fly everywhere. On the other hand, it has the advantage of being very dense, and thus comfortable for furniture and floor cushions, like the lounge cushion on page 113.

—Foam. Available from fabric stores or do-it-yourself shops. It comes in various densities and thicknesses, and can be cut into the shape you need. It works best for objects that need to hold their shape (as in the Moroccan pouffe on page 86) and is less suitable for things that should be soft and pliant.

• Embroidery Floss

I use various kinds of embroidery thread, either from necessity (some stitches don't lend themselves easily to some threads) or for aesthetic effect. DMC offers a wide range of types and colors.

In any case, you will need to use an embroidery needle with a large eye.

—Flower thread is soft, matt, and easy to use. DMC has discontinued its line of flower thread, but Ginnie Thompson flower thread can be obtained.

—Six-strand embroidery floss is glossier than flower thread. It is indispensable for making Maltese tassels. It comes with six strands together, but you can divide these strands for finer stitches.

—Pearl thread has a shimmering, opalescent quality.

Variations in floss type are sometimes suggested to change the effect of a project.

• Beads, Spangles, and Sequins

Raw or refined linen can be matched with all of these for a variety of effects. In projects such as the flower brooch on page 25, the macramé bracelets on page 29, and the umbel-motif stole on page 21, I suggest changing these ornaments for a completely different style.

• Leather

As well as smooth leathers like the one used for the Moroccan pouffe on page 86, you can also find patent leather, "distressed" leather, metallic leather, and waxed leather in specialty stores.

Leather is surprisingly easy to sew, with a sewing machine or by hand, as long as you use a thimble. Use needles and thread especially made for leather (available at all notions shops).

Embroidery Stitches

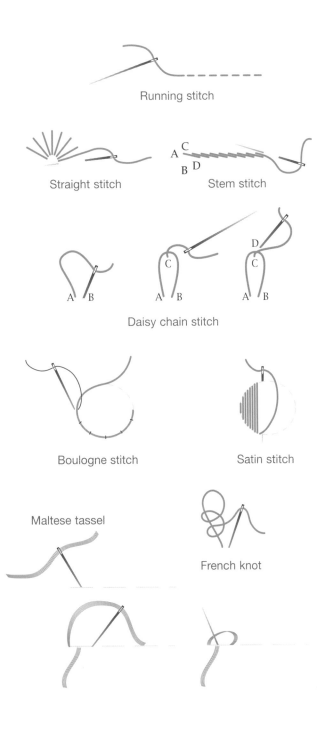

Running stitch

Straight stitch

Stem stitch

Daisy chain stitch

Boulogne stitch

Satin stitch

Maltese tassel

French knot

Running stitch

Straight stitch

Bringing the needle through from the right side of the fabric, sew stitches a few millimeters apart, as long as is needed for the design.

Stem stitch

Bringing the needle through at A, push it back in at B and bring it out again at C; Continue by pushing the needle back in at D.

Daisy chain stitch

This stitch is formed by a loop that is held at the top at one point: bring the needle out at the base of the "petal" at A and push it back in at B, keeping a loop of floss; bring it back out at the top at C, under the loop of floss; finally, push it back through at D, just above the loop.

Boulogne stitch

Bring a needle threaded with a strand of floss or raffia through to the right side of the piece of cloth being embroidered; arrange the floss or raffia in the desired shape on the cloth. Tack it down with small, regularly space stitches across the floss or raffia, using a needle threaded with beige thread. Push the needle with the floss or raffia through to the back of the cloth when the line is finished.

Satin stitch

Bring the needle out at the top and push it back through at the bottom, making the stitches parallel and touching each other, to fill in the desired form.

French knot

Bring the needle through to the front; with the left hand, pull the thread to the left and wind the needle once or twice around the thread you are holding, in a clockwise direction; push the needle back through, while holding the knot you've formed down tightly with your finger, very close to where you brought the thread out.

Maltese tassel

With a textile pen, draw a 6-mm line to mark the placement of each tassel.

Thread a needle with the six-strand embroidery floss, retaining all six strands.

Bring the needle through the middle of the marked line; pull the floss through, leaving a ¾-in. strand of thread. Bring the needle out again on the left side of the line, and enter again on the far right side underneath the strand. Bring it out again at the center.

Cut this second strand to the same length as the first. The 2 cm of floss that sticks out will make a little tassel.

Acknowledgments

I would especially like to thank:

La Societe Regards à Chinon, and especially their talented founders Jean-Baptiste Astier de Villatte and Gael Dechelette, for their warm reception;

Mr. and Mrs. Plumel, who have a wonderful garden;

Johanna Levy;

Sonia and Emmanuel Amara;

Jeannine Cros, whose sheets, tablecloths, and other antique textiles in their myriad hues are an absolute marvel;

Magali and her mother, for their charming relics of days gone by;

Patricia Chaveau, from Pebeo;

Jacqueline Mogne, from DMC;

My mother, for her help and her patience;

and Laetitia, Claire, Aurélie, Hugo, and Sandrine.